The Good, The Bad, and The Dirty Laundry

(Character traits found in the book of Esther)

The Laundry Lady
Leslie D. Dawes
www.thelaundrylady.org

ISBN: 978-0-578-00983-4

Copyright © 2002 by Leslie D. Dawes

All rights reserved. Written permission must be secured from the publisher to use or reproduce any part of this book, except for brief quotations in critical reviews or articles.

Scripture quotations are from the amplified version of the bible.

United States Copyright Office:
Dawes, Leslie
TXu001054204   2002-06-07

Table of Contents

Why "The Laundry Lady" 4
Dedication 5

Week 1:
Day 1 6
Day 2 11
Day 3 14
Day 4 18
Day 5 21

Week 2:
Day 1 25
Day 2 29
Day 3 33
Day 4 36
Day 5 39

Week 3:
Day 1 43
Day 2 47
Day 3 50
Day 4 54
Day 5 58

Week 4:
Day 1 62
Day 2 66
Day 3 69
Day 4 72
Day 5 75

Week 5:
Day 1 78
Day 2 81
Day 3 84
Day 4 87
Day 5 90

Week 6:
Day 1 92
Day 2 97
Day 3 100
Day 4 103
Day 5 106

Why "The laundry lady"

In the Fall of 2001 God spoke plain and clear on a school bus full of 4th grade students. Leslie, here is the lesson I have for you to make known for me. "**Laundry!**" I said "What, Lord?" He said, "Laundry!" "Okay, I will finish the laundry when I get home. I know I haven't kept up with it like I should," I responded.

He then began pouring into my heart the idea that our past hurts, present sufferings and future trials are laundry, specifically "dirty laundry" that he needs to work with to make useable for his glory.

With his guidance and a lot of time before him, he has carved a ministry to help women understand what God has planned for their lives and how the ugliest past can be a glorious offering of usefulness and purpose for Christ, if we only allow God to wash, dry, fold and properly put away the dirty laundry in our lives.

DEDICATION

To my precious husband that understands my heart for ministry and my love for the study of God's word.

Lovingly dedicated to my precious CHILDREN, without them I could not love Jesus the way I do.

Week 1 — Day 1 — King Xerxes

Read Esther Chapter 1:1-9

Laundry Basket: Esther 1:1-2
As we begin, we will be looking at the first character we are introduced to in the book of Esther, King Xerxes. In some translations he is called King Ahasuerus. Ahasuerus is a title. It would be like us calling someone Governor or President. This was an official title not his name.

He is the ruler of 127 provinces. Provinces were somewhat like counties. They were an area surrounding a city. They were marked out to help with the collecting of taxes and administrative tasks. These provinces stretched from India to Ethiopia. A vast area; some say he was the most powerful man in the world at the time.

Laundry Basket: Let's continue, read Esther 1:3-9

Laundry Lesson: Laundry, who likes doing dirty laundry? For me, it is one of the worse jobs in the house. It is an endless task that just never seems to be done. As soon as one stack is done another stack has formed; Endless, tiring and absolutely time consuming. But when we think about it, isn't that exactly how our besetting sin(s) is(are)? We spend all sorts of time, money and effort to cover up or make the sin okay. When the truth is, it is sin, and it needs to be dealt with. Are we willing to go there with God? Are we willing to allow God to uncover those areas in our lives that separate us from an open and full relationship with him? Let's allow God to transform us by learning from other's "dirty laundry."

Let's take a look at King Xerxes and his besetting sin of:

Dirty Laundry: "Use or Abuse of Power"

Can you imagine a party that lasted 180 days? This was a monstrous party; one that would turn every head; one that would prove that King Xerxes was the most important man in the land. This is exactly what the King wanted. Most researchers suggest he threw this party to show off his wealth and influence. He was trying to gain support because his plan was to invade Greece. This party served two purposes: 1) to intimidate the Greeks and 2) to encourage the troops before battle.

Let's capture the essence of his besetting sin. What is the cause of being "Power Hungry," and what is the consequence. Is there a better road? Yes!! Let's talk about that as well.

Laundry Detergent (God's Word):
"No king succeeds with a big army alone, no warrior wins by brute strength."
Psalm 33:16

What does this verse say to you: _____
_____

"True wisdom and real power belong to God, from him we learn how to live,
and what to live for." Job 12:13

Can we be leaders and not possess leadership? Yes or No and why_____
Leadership: a quality given by God, but if not controlled by God can be
disastrous. Have you been in leadership of any sort? _____
_____

It can bring with it a sense of "I know it all;" Making you feel more important
than you truly are. Is this at all what God intended when he designed us for
leadership? No! True leadership is found when the source of leadership is
Jesus; when we are just the hands and feet of leadership. Notice, I didn't say
the mouth piece of leadership. To often, the mouthpiece of leadership runs
before the actions of leadership ever surface. Leadership is a showing of
action, servant action. I have been told the sign of a good "leader" is that
things work just as smooth with the "leader" absent as with the "leader"
present. Meaning, the leader doesn't hold all the power the leader just
designates it.

King Xerxes believes he rules it all. His "power" had gone to his head. See
this story about the "Power" of King Xerxes:
    As recorded at "www.adam2.org" - It took Xerxes four years to plan
    and prepare for his massive invasion of Greece. From every corner of
    the Persian Empire, Xerxes collected vast quantities of food, money,
    and weapons, which he stockpiled for the impending conquest.
    Meanwhile, the Persian army honed its skills by putting down a
    rebellion in Egypt.
    Xerxes' army was the biggest that had ever been assembled in the
    ancient world, numbering at least several hundred thousand troops.
    The army's strongest regiment was an elite corps of ten thousand
    hand-picked warriors known as the Immortals. The greater part of the
    army was, however, drafted from the enslaved masses of the Persian
    Empire.

This army began marching toward Greece in the spring of 480 B.C. It took a full
week for the entire force to pass by any given point along the line of march.
    As the thirsty army passed through the countryside, springs, wells
    and small rivers along its route were frequently drunk dry.

Xerxes ordered a fleet of a thousand warships to sail along the coast of the Aegean Sea, following his army and carrying provisions for the long march to Greece.

Xerxes called a temporary halt when his army reached the stormy straits of the Dardanelles, at the mouth of the Black Sea. To transport his army across the mile-wide waterway, Xerxes sent hundreds of ships from his fleet into the channel, where they were tied together with thick ropes to create a floating bridge. A violent storm destroyed this bridge before the Persian army was able to cross it.

Enraged, Xerxes ordered that the waters of the Dardanelles be whipped and branded with hot irons. The soldiers sent to perform this symbolic act of punishment recited the following royal proclamation:

"O vile waterway! Xerxes lays on you this punishment because you have offended him, although he has done you no wrong! The great king Xerxes will cross you even without your permission, for you are a treacherous and foul river!"

Xerxes also put to death the engineers responsible for building the bridge. He then recruited a second team of bridge-builders, who cleverly decided to build two floating bridges, one for the use of the army's troops, and a second, downstream, which would carry the large herds of horses and other animals across the straits. The engineers also made sure to use thicker ropes to tie the ships together. After the ropes were pulled taut by giant windlasses anchored to either shore, mile-long embankments of timber, stone and packed earth were laid across the ships' decks to form roadways.

In the weeks that it took to assemble the floating bridges, Xerxes ordered his naval commanders to allow grain-ships bound for Greece to pass through the Dardanelles unharmed. "Are we not bound for the same destination?" he asked. "I do not see that those ships are doing us any harm by carrying our grain for us."

I know many of you, like me, are probably laughing at that story, but this is a true account of his belief that he was even better than the sea. What an abuse of his position.

God had placed him as the leader of a vast territory and a large group of people, among those people were a remnant of Jews. The Jews had been in exile for 80 years and had been allowed just a few years prior to return to Jerusalem. Some had not returned. This remnant was spread throughout several regions. There were several million Jews throughout the 127 provinces King Xerxes oversaw.

List those in your life that you oversee or have direct influence on:

_____   _____

_____   _____

_____   _____

List those in your life that you have indirect influence on:

_____   _____

_____   _____

_____   _____

Laundry Detergent (God's Word): Fill in the blanks.

Psalm 139:23 _____ me, O God, and know my heart; try me, and know my _____.

Exodus 9:16 But indeed for this _____ I have raised **you** up, that I may show my _____ in **you**, and that My name may be _____ in all the earth.

Is there an area in my life Lord that I am "too big for my britches?" _____
_____

Is there someone in my life that has been hurt or turned away from you because of my attitude or actions? _____

What are 3 specifics I can do to keep my "power" or "leadership" in perspective?

- _____
- _____
- _____

Steam Cleaned:

Lord, help me today to turn from abusing power that you have graciously given me. May I humble myself before you and be grateful for the opportunity to lead others to you by influencing them for you. Reveal to me actions or attitudes that may be hindering your work in their lives. Help me to be ever open to your working. Keep my feet planted firmly on the rock of your truth.

In Jesus Name, Amen

Each day there will be a personal evaluation topic that will be addressed. It will be in the form of a question. Spend time with God evaluating your heart and motive in each area. Use the space provided to write notes, prayer requests or needs.

Dirty Laundry (Personal Evaluation):
Whom has God put in my life to oversee and I just "abuse the power" given to me and just push my way around?

Week 1 – Day 2 – King Xerxes

Read Esther 1:4-2:4

Laundry Basket: Esther 1:10-21
This part of the book of Esther always brings a smile to my face. The thought of a grown man, rich, no doubt popular and **skunk drunk**. He is so full of himself he makes a request that, in his right mind, he never would have made. In his right mind, he would have beheaded someone for coming up with such an idea.

Laundry Lesson: Ever put to much detergent into a load of laundry. Well, it doesn't always happen like on TV and bubbles come pouring out of the washing machine, sometimes, the soap just builds up in the clothes. Once the clothes are put in the dryer or hung out to dry the soap just gets stiff. Then the clothes are uncomfortable and can sometimes cause skin rashes. Pride is that way too. If we don't choose to humble ourselves before God and realize the truth: "You are my Lord; I have no good besides You." (Psalm 16:2), we will become puffed up and believe to highly of ourselves. We will become stiff necked and become irritating to those around us.

Dirty Laundry: Pride

Let's slow down and get a good picture of the scene. King Xerxes has been throwing a party for 180 days for the noblemen (important people) of the provinces. Now, immediately he throws a 7 day party for everyone who wants to come. He is reclining amongst his guests, drinking as he wishes, having a merry ole time; in other words drinking himself stupid: when a thought hits him. "I have the most beautiful wife in the kingdom. I will show everyone. Hey, Mr. Eunuch, go tell Vashti to come in here naked. Oh, tell her to wear her crown so everyone knows who she is. I want everyone to see her." Okay, even in our culture, **stupid request**. Vashti refuses to do what her drunken husband requests and King Xerxes throws a temper tantrum. After consulting with a bunch of other drunken men, they determine that if Vashti won't obey King Xerxes, then the other wives won't obey their husbands so King Xerxes has her dethroned.

After yesterday's lesson and the story about King Xerxes having the sea spanked and today's lesson about Vashti, we would all agree that the King has a pride problem. He believes he should always get his way and because he makes the laws; they should all be in his favor. So, we should take notice that he could have had Vashti killed, but apparently he did have feelings for her because he only had her removed from the throne and banned from ever entering his presence again.

List your gifts and talents:

_____   _____
_____   _____
_____   _____

Have any of these areas become an area of pride? Yes or No? Why? _____
_____

Laundry Detergent (God's Word): Fill in the blanks.
Psalm 10:4 in his _____ the _____ does not see Him, in all his _____ there is no room for _____.

Proverbs 29:23 a man's _____ will bring him _____, but a _____ spirit will obtain _____.

1 Peter 5:6 _____ yourself under God's mighty hand, the He may _____ you up in _____ _____.

What should humbleness look like in our lives?
- Putting others before myself
- Bowing our heads and hearts to God
- Staying prayerfully connected to God's way of thinking and reacting.

What are 3 specifics I can do to put humbleness into practice in my life?
- _____
- _____
- _____

Steam Cleaned:
Lord, I realize outside of you, I am nothing. You knew me before I was born and you know my heart. You gave me the gifts and talents that I have and you want me to use them for your glory. Please help me bow my knee to your authority. Help me submit to you so that your love and light can show through me to others around. If I have offended someone with a prideful attitude please reveal it to me so that I can make it right with them. Help me to see myself through the cross and not standing on my own. Cause me to be humbled by the grace it took and continues to take in my life. May your name be praised!!
Amen

Dirty Laundry (Personal Evaluation):

What gifts or talents (even spiritual gifts) do I have that I have allowed to become an area of pride? Am I hard to live with because I have to have my way? Have I turned someone away from God because of my prideful attitude? Have I missed God's voice because I have not bowed my knee to his authority?

Week 1 — Day 3 — King Xerxes

Read Esther 1:10-22

Laundry Lesson: As a child, ever spill anything on your clothes and your mother say "Better get that washed out before that stain sets." If a stain sets in clothes it is almost impossible to get it out. The garment is ruined. You can scrub, use all sorts of products but there is always a residue left over. This is the way bitterness is in our lives. If we allow anger to take root it will grow into bitterness; once set, it is next to impossible to get bitterness out of your heart. With a lot of hard work bitterness can be beaten but there is a residue whether in our lives or the lives of others. How careful we need to be not to allow bitterness to set up in our lives.

Dirty Laundry: Anger

Laundry Basket: Esther 1:12
We talked a little about this yesterday but I wanted to dive into this deeper today.

We've established that King Xerxes has a pride problem. We want to see how many other sins can be attached to pride. You can multiple sins by hundreds when pride is at the root. Let's look at King Xerxes as an example:

He is having a party to prove he is important (pride). Then he ask his wife to show off her beauty (pride – remember at this time a wife was property, not a partner). She refuses, he gets mad. He doesn't get his way so he gets angry.

Xerxes was a man of power and influence so he could react anyway he wanted. This had been the case most of his life. His father was the King before him, so he had grown up in a life of power. That power had set in his heart incorrectly so it became pride and therefore anything that went against his wishes resulted in anger.

Key: We need to search our hearts to see that anytime we find ourselves reacting in anger, could pride be at the root?

Let's continue. Also, we read the story on Day One about King Xerxes' having the sea spanked because it went against his army. He had been allowed to act and react without any accountability for so long that any tantrum was not dealt with. This is a very volatile man.

Verse 12 reads, "the King became <u>furious </u>and <u>burned</u> with anger.

If we were to put the meanings of these words into this verse it would read like this:

"The King was showing a <u>burst of rage</u> and his <u>poison of anger and hot displeasure seared</u> in him."

This probably looked a lot like a three year old temper tantrum. We would want to put a quick halt to a tantrum like this in our children. That would be training them in self-control. We would also be wise to train ourselves in self-control. Anger is normally a sign of underlying issues. Meaning, there is something more at the heart. Not just, I'm mad. So don't just write anger off as a sin unto itself. It is one that needs self-examination. If anger is not dealt with it will become bitterness. Bitterness is like a root system. It grows out, around, down, over, under and in everything. It begins to affect every other area of our lives. We tend to think everyone is out to get us. It just becomes life-invading.

What particular things set you off? Are they areas that need to be surrendered?

Laundry Detergent (God's Word): Fill in the blanks. There is a space provided after each verse to make note of any warning signs that would help control or alleviate our battle with anger.

Proverbs 15:1 A _____ answer turns away _____, but a harsh word stirs up _____.
- _____

Proverbs 15:18 A _____ man stirs up _____, but a _____ man calms a _____.
- _____

Proverbs 16:32 Better a _____ man than a warrior, a man who _____ his _____ than one who takes a city.
- _____

Proverbs 19:11 A man's _____ gives him; it is to his _____ to overlook an _____.
- _____

Ecclesiastes 7:9 Do not be quickly _____ in your spirit, for _____ resides in the lap of _____.
- _____

Ephesians 4:31-32 get rid of all _____, rage and _____, brawling and _____, along with every form of malice. Be kind and compassionate to one another, forgiving each other, just as in Christ God forgave you.

- _____

God's word is so rich with scripture that it speaks clearly on keeping our hearts clear and free from anger and bitterness, we would be wise to study on a regular basis the "topic" of anger.

What are 3 specifics based on the truths found today that I can do to bring my anger under God's direction and daily control?

- _____
- _____
- _____

Steam Cleaned:

Lord, my heart, only you can know. There are places that I have hidden from even myself. Search my heart for any anger that is lurking in the deepest areas and bring them into your glorious light. Cause me to know the truth about how anger and bitterness can destroy my life and those around me. How it can destroy relationships. Penetrate the hardest parts and help me find safety and comfort in you. If my anger is justified help me stand on the truth of your word that "you oh Lord are my shield and defense" and that you will make right the wrongs done against me.

In Jesus Name,

Amen

Dirty Laundry (Personal Evaluation):
What are things that make me mad? Does my life exhibit signs of bitterness? Am I hard to live with because of my anger problem?

Week 1 — Day 4 — Queen Vashti

Read Esther 1:9-22

Laundry Basket: Esther 1:11-12
Queen Vashti has refused to do something that may cost her everything, including her life. To refuse an order of the King is no small matter. But let's look deeper. The King had asked her to come wearing nothing but her crown. He was asking her to walk around naked in front of a crowd of drunken men. Imagine the decision she had to make: Do I risk my life for this, or do I just go ahead and hope none of them remember this when they sober up? No! Her decision was not based on what the outcome would be. Her decision was based on her conviction; a heart decision that had been made earlier.

Laundry Lesson: Have you ever stood and watched the washers at the Laundromat? When they are in the wash cycle, how the clothes are tossed round and round, back and forth. It looks as if they are being beaten. The soap is foaming the washer is shaking and making all sorts of horrible noises. Life sometimes feels this way. When we have to take a stand for a personal conviction in our lives, it may feel like we have been thrown square into a "Wishy-Washy" (as Big Mama would call it) washer. It can cause us to question whether we have understood scripture correctly. It may even be well meaning Christians that are up against us in the struggle. But remember, scripture says that we "are hard pressed on every side, yet not crushed; we are perplexed, but not in despair; persecuted, but not forsaken; struck down, but not destroyed – (II Corinthians 4:8-9)

Laundry: Personal Convictions

There is no other record of Queen Vashti. There are no stories in the chronicles of the King. There are no historical records about her. The only story we have is the one recorded in the book of Esther.

We see 3 things that she exhibited in her decision that would help when we need to take a stand in a conviction that God has place on our hearts.

1. Her convictions were established prior to the situations
    a. Our convictions <u>are not</u> situation based. They are personal belief based, that is established during a teaching time or learning moment with God or an authority figure.
    b. These are hearts issues, they are not situation ethics. These type convictions, those that you would stake your life on, are not those that you are willing to change according to the circumstances.

2. Popularity or lack of it was not her concern.
    a. Our personal convictions may or may not make us popular.
    b. We have to be satisfied that we are popular with God.
3. The outcome did not matter to Vashti.
    a. Our focus must be on obedience, not on the consequences.
    b. We must remember God is our defense he will make the wrongs, right.

List some of the personal convictions that you will not budge on:

_____   _____

_____   _____

_____   _____

Read: Romans 14:12-22. This passage of scripture is a great picture of personal conviction. God may call some of us to live a life different than others. That's God's call!!!!! We are to live the life that God has called us to and to stand on the truths he has stated in his word. We are not to waver from our convictions. That does not mean that our convictions are to become others convictions. We must be careful. ***Jesus is the only Savior and Lord***!!! That is the truth. That is not a conviction. Some examples of conviction are: *I don't eat meat because I believe God wouldn't have me to eat meat. *I home school my children because God wants me to do that. *I don't go to the movie theater to watch movies because I believe God wouldn't want me to do that.

Laundry Detergent (God' Word): Fill in the blanks.
Romans 14:22 so whatever you _____ about these things keep between yourself and _____. _____ is the man who does not _____ himself by what he approves.

What are 3 areas, God prompted, that you have not established as non-negotiable in your life:

- _____
- _____
- _____

Steam Cleaned:

Lord, I want to be a person that stands for you. I want people to know that your ways and your word are my guideline. Please help me to examine my heart and allow you to establish within me truths that do not change with the situation. Help me obey regardless of the consequences. I want my life to honor you.

In Jesus Name, Amen

Dirty Laundry (Personal Evaluation):
Do I have personal convictions or situational ethics? Do I compromise clear biblical principles for popularity? Am I passing biblical truths to my children so that they become convictions in their lives?

Week 1 — Day 5 — King Xerxes

Read Esther Chapter 2

Laundry Basket: Esther 2:1-4

The time period between Chapter 1 and Chapter 2 is about three years. Xerxes has returned from his battle with Greece. His troops have been defeated. He is feeling sorry for himself. Then scripture states in verse 1 "he remembered Vashti and what she had done and what he had decreed about her." He was experiencing "regret." He recalls his actions and remembers that he was drunk and in haste made a decision that would affect him for the rest of his life.

Laundry Lesson: Ever had a bleach stain on a pair of jeans. I know you can buy them like that now, but I am talking about a bleach spot that was caused by coming in contact with bleach. The spot looks different than the rest of the garment. It stands out. It draws attention to itself because it's so different. When you wear that pair of jeans you feel as if everyone is staring at that spot. This is how regret works in our life. It is like a stain on our hearts. We feel like everyone can see the regret written on our face (and sometimes they can). It continues to draw attention to itself in our lives. It is so different than anything else in our hearts that it just stands out in our minds. God doesn't want us to live a life of regret.

Dirty Laundry: Regret

There are two kinds of regret:
1. Regret brought on by something someone did to us.
2. Regret brought on by something we did ourselves.

Regret brought on by someone else in our lives is dealt with more on the side of our emotional reaction to the situation. Anger, bitterness, forgiveness are all a part of that process.

Regret brought on by our own actions is something totally different. This regret is what leaves the stain on our hearts that Satan can use against us if we don't properly deal with it.

Guilt is a major component of regret. Have you ever noticed the mental battle that takes place in your mind with the onset of regret? How you can begin to think all sorts of "bad" thoughts about yourself and how you get on the mental treadmill of "What if...?", or "I should have...!" It can be very draining mentally. The bible never uses the term "regret" but there is an example in scripture that I believe will help us work through regret that is invading our minds.

Laundry Basket: Psalm 51
This chapter of scripture is written by David not long after his life altering events with Bathsheba. Remember the story: David is on the roof of his house looks over and sees Bathsheba taking a bath on the roof of her house. He begins to lust after her. Sends one of his servants to get her; spends the night with her. She becomes pregnant, so to hide his sin, he had her husband sent to the front line of the war and he is killed. He thinks no one knows until God sends the prophet Nathan to confront him. David writes Psalm 51 after this has taken place.

David's correct dealing with regret lead to his restoration and thus he was able to continue to be used by God.

We must note: Satan does not want us to deal with regret. This is a great hindrance to our spiritual growth and a relationship strain with God.

Make a list of situations that you are dealing with regret over:
- † _____
- † _____
- † _____

Laundry Detergent (God's Word): Fill in the blanks.

Psalm 51:4: Against you, you only, have I _____, and done what is _____ in your sight, so that you are proved right when you speak and _____ when you _____.
- Acknowledge personal responsibility. Sometimes the hardest part of dealing with regret.
  Notes for personal acknowledgement of responsibility:
  _____
  _____

- Truth to renew the "foothold" in your heart:
  Notes for personal renewing of the heart and scripture reference for the replacing the foothold of regret:
  _____
  _____

Psalm 51:10: _____ in me a pure _____, O God, and _____ spirit within me.

   Renewing of the heart: Allowing God to replace regret with a so[...] basis.

Psalm 51:12: _____ to me the joy of your _____ grant me a _____ spirit, to _____ me.
- Restoration comes from accepting God's forgiveness and applying [...] forgiveness to the "regret" spot in your heart.
  Notes for personal restoration of regret spot:

  _____
  _____

Psalm 51:14: _____ me from bloodguilt, O God, the God who sav[...] me, and my _____ will sing of your _____.
- Deliverance from any thoughts of regret or guilt. Asking God to bring deliverance from the mental treadmill that is associated with guilt. The consequences of sin will remain but the guilt and regret should not remain.
  Notes for personal deliverance of regret:

  _____
  _____

Psalm 51:15-17: O Lord, _____ my lips and my _____ will declare your _____. You do not _____ in _____, or I would bring it; you do not take _____ in burnt offerings. The _____ of God are a _____ spirit; a _____ and _____ heart, O God, you will not _____.
- Praise and worship should be a natural outpouring of God's work of restoration.

Write a "psalm" of praise and thanksgiving for the healing of regret:

_____
_____
_____
_____
_____
_____
_____

Steam Cleaned:

Lord, please help me to rest in the restoration you bring. Help me not to run from the healing and renewing that only you can give. Lord, please free my heart from regret. Help me to allow you to "wash, dry, fold" and make useful the areas that Satan wanted to use to hold me back from all that you have planned for me.

In Jesus Name,

Amen.

How does a worm get in an apple? Perhaps you think the worm burrows in from the outside. No, scientists have discovered that the worm comes from the inside. But how does it get in there? Simple. An insect lays an egg in the apple blossoms. The apple develops around the egg. Sometime later the worm hatches in the heart of the apple and burrows his way out! SIN, like the worm, BEGINS in the HEART and works out through the person's THOUGHTS, WORDS and ACTIONS. For this reason, David once wrote, "Create in me a clean heart, O God."

Dirty Laundry (Personal Evaluation):

Is there a "regret" situation I am dwelling on in my heart and mind? Is "regret" invading my every thought and action? Is "regret" affecting my relationship with God? Am I allowing Satan that foothold in my heart?

Week 2 — Day 1 — Esther

Read Esther Chapter 2

Laundry Basket: Esther 2:8-23
Hadassah a girl between the ages of 15-22; adopted by her cousin because her father and mother die, destined to be an old maid (Sounds like Cinderella story). Her world changes when the king sends out a decree. Officers come. They inspect the daughters of each house. Those they believe to be "beautiful" are taken to the palace.

Laundry Lesson: Do you know what to do if you find chewing gum stuck to the drum of your dryer? I didn't, until gum was stuck to the drum of my dryer. I had to search the internet and ask my friends. It took research and a willingness to learn and be taught. That's how we should be as Christians also; always ready to be taught by someone who knows better, someone wiser, someone to teach us the truths of God's word.

Laundry: Meekness & Teachable Spirit

Verse 9 states: *"The girl pleased him and won his favor."*

So even before Esther becomes Queen she is given special treatment. She is given 7 maidens of her own. She is given the best room in the house. She is given extra beauty treatments. She stood out from the rest. Could this be just outward beauty? There were approximately 1500 girls there. Here we have an everyday girl ripped from her family and brought to a place where she knows no one and can not control anything that happens and she shines with Godly character.

Look at verse 15: *When the turn came for Esther (the girl Mordecai had adopted, the daughter of his uncle Ablhail) to go to the king, she asked for nothing other than what Hegai, the king's eunuch who was in charge of the harem, suggested.*

While this rivalry for the position of queen is going on, here's Hadassah making friends. Everyone likes her and favors her. She is beautiful but teachable. She is treated differently but she is humble. She has her pick of anything she wants to take with her to the king but she obeys Hegai and takes his advice. Hadassah is well suited for the roll of queen. Hadassah had a teachable spirit. She was willing to learn. She understood that Hegai knew best. Because of her willingness to submit to Hegai she was crowned queen. What an incredible thing has happened to this young woman. She was an **orphan**. Now, she's **queen**! Isn't that just like God?

We may not be Queen but we are royalty. We are daughters of the King of Kings. Don't you think it's time we started acting like it?

What female traits do you see in Hadassah that you would like to cultivate in your life:

_____ _____
_____ _____
_____ _____

Laundry Detergent (God's Word): Fill in the blanks.

Ecclesiastes 8:1: Who is like the _____ man? Who knows the _____ of things? _____ brightens a man's face and _____ its hard _____.

Galatians 5:22-25 But the fruit of the Spirit is love, joy, peace, patience, kindness, goodness, faithfulness, _____ and _____. Against such things there is no law. Those who belong to Christ Jesus have crucified the sinful nature with its passions and desires. Since we live by the Spirit, let us _____ _____ _____ with the Spirit. Let us not become _____, _____ and _____ each other.

Colossians 3:12: Therefore, as God's chosen people, _____ and _____ _____, clothe yourselves with _____, _____, _____, _____ and _____.

James 1:21: Therefore, get rid of all _____ _____ and the evil that is so prevalent and humbly accept the word planted in you, which can save you.

James 3:13: Who is _____ and _____ among you? Let him show it by his _____ _____, by deeds done in the humility that comes from _____.

Psalm 22:26: The _____ will eat and be _____; they who _____ the Lord will _____ him – may your hearts live forever!

Psalm 25:9: He guides the _____ in what is right and _____ them his way.

Note 3 steps, prompted by God, to take to establish humility, meekness and teachable ness:

- _____
- _____
- _____

Steam Cleaned:

Lord, please help me to cultivate humbleness and teachable ness in my life. Help me to live a life controlled by the spirit so that I may walk in such a way that my life would cause me to find favor with those that I come in contact with. Please help me seek meekness, and seek your face. Show me areas where I do not honor you with my actions.

In Jesus Name,
Amen.

Dirty Laundry (Personal Evaluation):
Do I get mad when someone tries to teach me something? Do I think I know it all?
Do I always have to have my way? Is my only way of learning the - "trial and error"
– method?

Week 2— Day 2 — Esther

Read Esther Chapter 2

Laundry Basket: Esther 2:19-20

What does honor mean anyway? **RESPECT**! Plain and simple.

Honoring our parents as adults is one of those things that can become tricky. How far do we go to do what they ask before they are asking too much? How much time spent with them is right? When do we interrupt what they are saying when it doesn't match what we teach our children?

Laundry Lesson: Ever read the directions on the back of the Fabric softener sheet box? Me either. We tend to try things our way before we read the directions. We don't read the directions until something goes wrong. We are like this when we deal with our parents also. We tend to believe that we know better than they do. We have to train ourselves to honor our parents' requests and their advice.

Laundry: Honoring your Father and Mother

There seems to be a fine line to walk when honoring our parents but we are to do this. Parents are God's gift to us to help us navigate life. Parents instruct, comfort, love unconditionally and watch over the actions, reactions and activities of their children.

Esther is a wonderful example of how honoring your parent even in adulthood is God honoring also. She recognizes the wisdom of Mordecai and listens to his counsel. She pays careful attention, even in the face of death, to the instructions of her father.

Look at this next section; it is from sermon by John Hammond:

"Honor your father and mother" was not originally so much about children sassing their parents as about providing respect and care for older people. The command was not primarily written to minors. This command is for adults to heed. The original context suggests that children should be sure to take care of their aged parents when they are feeble and no longer able to take care of themselves. In our culture, the expectation is that our parents will work till they are wealthy and can retire, and then when they die, they leave us an inheritance.

But this is an exception, not the norm for most cultures. For most cultures, there comes a time when elderly parents can no longer work, and meet their own needs. That's when children need to remember God's command with a promise. Honor your parents. Given this understanding, this German folktale is a commentary on the Fourth Commandment:

There was once a couple who lived with their only son Conrad in a modest house at the edge of a great forest. Though they were not rich, they lived a comfortable and happy life together. One day the man's father came to make his home with the young couple. The old grandfather's eyes had grown dim, his ears nearly deaf, and his hands shook like leaves in the wind. When he ate he was unable to hold his spoon without spilling food on the tablecloth and the floor. Often bits of food would run out of his mouth, soiling his clothing. For months the young couple discussed the irritating behavior of the old man. Finally they set a table for him to eat in a corner of the kitchen. As he ate, he looked sadly at his family. When he spilt his food, he would sob.
Finally one day the old man's trembling hands could no longer hold the glass bowl, and it fell to the floor, breaking into a dozen pieces. The woman scolded him and immediately went to the market where she purchased a wooden bowl for the grandfather. As the days passed the old man said very little as he sat in his corner eating out of his wooden bowl. Late in the fall the father came home from a long day's work to find Conrad sitting in the middle of the floor carving a block of wood. "What are you making, my young man?" asked the father. "It is a present for you and mommy," answered the child. "I am carving two wooden bowls so that you will have something to eat from when you live with me in your old age." The husband and wife looked at each other for a long time, and finally they began to weep. That evening they moved the old grandfather back to the family table. From that day on he always ate with them, and they said nothing even when he spilled his food.

Why obey and honor your parents? Because it is right!

Areas you should honor your parents:

---------------------   ---------------------
---------------------   ---------------------
---------------------   ---------------------

Laundry Detergent (God's Word): Fill in the blanks.

Exodus 20:12: Honor your _____ and your _____, so that you may _____ long in the land the LORD your God is _____ you.

Deuteronomy 5:16: Honor your father and your mother, as the _____ _____ _____ has commanded you, so that you may live long and that it may _____ _____ with you in the land the LORD your God is giving you.

Matthew 15:4: For God said, Honor your father and mother' and _____ who curses his father or mother must be put to _____.

Matthew 19:19: Jesus replied, Do not murder, do not commit adultery, do not steal, do not give false testimony, _____ your _____ and _____, and love your neighbor as yourself.

Ephesians 6:2: "Honor your father and mother"—which is the _____ commandment with a _____-

How we need to carefully consider the words we use and the heart attitude we have when we approach our parents. Speaking from experience there will come a day when a phone call, a hug or a pat on the back will be greatly missed. The day will come when that parent will no longer be on this earth. It will come all too quickly. Respect your parents what a legacy to leave your children.

What 3 things will you do this week to honor your parents:
- _____
- _____
- _____

Steamed Cleaned:

Father, help me to remember that my parents were chosen for me by you. You knew me before I was formed so you knew the best choice of parents for me. You had the perfect family and the perfect parents picked for me. Help me honor them because they are your choice. Remind me to take good care of them and help them when they are older. Help me not to take my parents and their wisdom for granted. May my words and deeds toward my parents be respectful and loving all of my days.

In Jesus Name,

Amen

Dirty Laundry (Personal Evaluation):
Do I "trash talk" my parents? Do I honor my parents in word and deed? Even as an adult, do I talk back to my parents? Do I listen to their wise counsel? Are my children able to learn respect and honor by watching how I treat my parents?

Week 2 — Day 3 — Haman

Read Esther Chapter 3

Laundry Basket: Esther 3:2-15
Verse 8 we find Haman begins his deception. He is a liar. He is not telling the King the whole truth. He tells the king enough to get the king's attention. Notice how Haman made it sound as if these people were doing the king wrong. This was not about the king at all. Haman lays his trap. Which brings us to the other trait we find in verses 7-9; he is a schemer. He manipulates people to get his way. What a dangerous person he is.

Laundry Lesson: Ever tried a new laundry detergent because the commercial said it was "new" or "improved" or "gets stains out better?" Did you find out later the commercial lied? Well, life is this way too. People lie. We live in a world where we are skeptical about anything anyone tells us because we have been lied to so many times.

Dirty Laundry: Lying

Lying at age 3 we call it – fibs. At age 12 we call them little white lies. In adulthood we say we are stretching the truth. Why don't we ever just call it what it is - **"Lying!"**

Who are we associating ourselves with when we lie according to John 8:44?

What does Colossians 3:9 say about lying?

Scripture does not categorize lies. There is no "little white lie" or "fib". They all come straight from the pit. Isn't that convicting? Even the half truths we tell are nothing but filth to the almighty God.

List personal areas in which it is hard to tell the truth:

--------------------   --------------------
--------------------   --------------------
--------------------   --------------------

Laundry Detergent: Acts 5:1-10

What was the sin of Ananias and Sapphira?

What was the punishment for their sin?

Why do you feel that God dealt so harshly with their sin?

_____

List 3 steps based on your truths found in scripture that you plan to make to live a life of personal truthfulness:

- --
- --
- --

Steam Cleaned:

Lord, my heart is deceptively wicked. I know that within myself I don't have the power to be completely truthful. I know that it takes the power of the Holy Spirit to be completely honest about all of my dealings with everyone in my life. Please help me be honest with you and with those around me.

In Jesus Name,

Amen.

Dirty Laundry (Personal Evaluation):

Are there things in your life that you need to confess to God? He already knows them. It will do you good to release them to him. Are there confessions that need to be made to someone around you? Have you been deceptive in business practices? Have you hidden something from a friend or family member that you shouldn't? Have you lied to your boss at work to get a promotion or a raise? Do you always tell the truth?

Week 2 — Day 4 — Mordecai

Read Esther Chapter 3

Laundry Basket: Esther 3:2-5

There is a phrase that we need to look at closely. It appears in verse 4 "to see whether Mordecai's behavior would be tolerated, for he had told them he was a Jew." Tolerated here means – confirm, continue, establish, stand firm, stand fast, stay or endure, trustworthy. They were making sure he would not waver in his faithfulness to the God he professed. Mordecai knew the one true and living God and he knew that he was not to bow or worship anyone or anything else.

Laundry Lesson: Ever bought "extra heavy starch?" You need your clothes to look extra good for a special occasion, so you starch them heavy so they will remain stiff and perfectly pressed all evening. Faithfulness should be like this in our lives. Something that is sure from early morning to late in the evening.

Laundry: Faithfulness

The word "faithful" is found 88 times throughout scripture. 22 of the 37 times faithful is used in the Old Testament it means "to trust or believe, or to be permanent or turn to the right."

With an architectural degree, the first thing that came to mind as I read the definition "to be permanent" was concrete. Concrete is not at its strongest when it is first set. The longer concrete is left the stronger it becomes. Years won't erode it. Time only makes it stronger. That is how our "faithfulness" to God should be; ever strengthening, ever trustworthy.

Faithfulness in my life is being molded once again: As I write this my uncle is in Room 4215 at Centennial Hospital in Nashville, Tennessee. He is a pancreatic cancer patient on the ICU floor. He has been battling this disease for 14 months and we have been on many hospital stays before. This one will be our last. He has been in the hospital 16 days so far this time. I have been spending the days there to help my aunt out and going home in the evenings to be a wife and mother. I have been struggling over this lesson. It has taken days to write a few sentences. As I was driving the 25 miles, for the 16th day in a row, to the hospital today, I was praying again, "God, I need you to speak to me. I need to know what you want to teach me about faithfulness." His response was, "Just be listening, my child." After being in the hospital room for a few hours, wiping my uncles forehead, swabbing out his dry mouth, helping him turn over and holding his hand. The affects of the morphine had him so confused and disoriented that he could not even hold his head up on his own. I began to get very weary. I began to weep. I was literally watching cancer steal my uncle away from me. He was physically heavy. He doesn't rest. It's a constant strain. I have two small children at home that do not understand that mommy is tired when she gets home. Just absolutely at the end of me but unwilling to stop because of the love I have for my uncle and aunt. God spoke, "This is faithfulness; "Just doing the right thing, at the right time, for the right reason; sticking to it even though it is hard and heartbreaking." My uncle is not expected to make it to many more days but until he goes home to be with his Jesus, I will be faithful to him and my aunt. Perseverance; Nothing about desire, emotion, or popularity; <u>It's all about just continuing to do what you know is right.</u>

In our relationship with God, faithfulness is the same. Continuing to believe and trust even though at time it seems it's the hardest thing to do; knowing that God is true to his word. "All things work together for good, to them that love God and are called according to his purpose." Faithfulness – Just continuing to – Study, Pray, Trust and Believe.

List areas where you lack faithfulness:

_____   _____
_____   _____
_____   _____

Laundry Detergent (God's Word): Fill in the blanks. Faithful or trustworthy is the word we are looking for in the following verses.

Proverbs 25:13: Like the coolness of snow at harvest time is a _____ messenger to those who send him; he _____ the spirit of his masters.

Matthew 25: 23: His master replied, "Well done, good and _____ servant! You have been _____ with a few things; I will put you in _____ of many things. Come and share your master's _____!

List 3 steps you can take to make faithfulness a part of your daily life:
- _____
- _____
- _____

Steam Cleaned:
Oh Jesus, how I want my life to be a picture of faithfulness to those around me. I want to be a trustworthy servant of yours. I want my every word and action to be faithful and sure. Make my paths straight and my heart focused on you. Thank you for your strength and direction.

In your precious Name, Amen

Dirty Laundry (Personal Evaluation):
Does my talk match my walk? Is faithfulness prevalent in my life?

Week 2 – Day 5 – King Xerxes

Read Esther Chapter 3

Laundry Basket: Esther 3:10-11
Not much interest by the King, two verses written about the King's involvement in the annihilation of an entire race of people; a race of people totaling 15 million in his empire. No meetings. No committees. No checking into the details. Just "do it!"

Laundry Lesson: Did you realize you can stop the washer before the rinse cycle. The clothes won't know the difference. You can even go ahead and dry, fold and put away the clothes and they still won't realize you didn't rinse them. The soap won't mind either. But put those same clothes on and almost immediately your skin will be aware that the clothes were not rinsed. You will break out in a rash and begin to itch. No relief will come until you change into some "clean" clothes. That's how our lives are when we live them unaware. We sail along, no cares. Then a spiritual attack hits and we are totally caught off guard. We begin to "itch" spiritually. We become uncomfortable in the "skin" we are living in. We beg for relief from God because we were not prepared to stand when the attack hit.

Dirty Laundry: Unaware

The King doesn't care what Haman is doing. He just trusts him. His gives him the most valuable article in the kingdom, his signet ring. The ring was used to seal any legal document. Anything bearing the seal of that signet ring was *irreversible* law, and the King just hands it over. Unbelievable!!!!

We as Christians are not to live life unaware. We are to keep our guard up at all times. It's hard to do. It is not a natural thing. It is something we must practice until it becomes natural "habit." Satan wants us to fall prey to him. Being unaware gives him the opportunity to devour us.

I Peter 5:8 says *"Be self-controlled and alert. Your enemy the devil prowls around like a roaring lion looking for someone to devour.*

The word of God plainly states that Satan doesn't just want us injured, he wants us devoured. He wants to engulf us, have us so entangled in his schemes that we can't see the light of day but we are to be alert: sober, vigilant, watchful

In self-defense they teach you color codes to correspond to different stages of awareness. White signifies no awareness. Orange means you know what is around you. Yellow is paying close attention to everyone and everything moving about. Knowing what is happening. Red means you feel threatened or in danger. Black is where you must defend yourself. You are in a situation where you must use resources to protect yourself. In this system, you always want to be at yellow to orange stages so that red or black is never an issue. If you are always paying attention, looking around, watching those around you then you have an opportunity to avoid situation that would cause you to need to defend yourself. If you walk around in stage white, you are an easy target.

We could use the same analogy with Christianity. If we walk through life with our spiritual eyes shut to God's working or Satan's schemes we will not only miss awesome times of seeing God but we will find ourselves entrapped in the snares of Satan time and time again. We can arm ourselves against Satan's devices. We can become more aware of God's plan.

Mention times when you know that you have been caught spiritually unaware:

----------------------- -----------------------
----------------------- -----------------------
----------------------- -----------------------

Laundry Detergent (God's Word):
Ephesians 6:11-18

Each piece of armor has a corresponding Christ-like attribute. Take a look:
Truth – God's Word
Righteousness – equity of character
Preparation – awareness
Faith – assurance, belief
Salvation – Christ as Savior
Word of God – Memorized Scripture

This armor protects us against being unaware. Our society even recognizes the importance of awareness. Think about it: Drug abuse awareness, Breast Cancer awareness, Domestic abuse awareness. We hear about awareness all the time. Let's focus our awareness where it should be: on the truth of God's word and his ways.

Let's have a little bit of fun that will help remind us to put on our armor when we are getting ready in the mornings.

For every piece of armor let's give it a corresponding article of clothing. Let's pretend we are career women. We are getting dress for work. Write the article of clothing that you would associate with the piece of armor that we need to put on:

Loins girded with truth	=	_____
Breastplate of righteousness	=	_____
Feet shod with the Gospel	=	_____
Shield of faith	=	_____
Helmet of Salvation	=	_____
Sword of the Spirit	=	_____

Don't miss the one that is the glue that holds the whole thing together *"praying always with all prayer and supplication in the spirit, and watching thereunto with all perseverance and supplication for all saints."*

We need to pray to stay aware. We can't just do our 5 minute devotion and expect that our armor will stay in tacked all day. We get hit with a few fiery darts from the enemy and then our shield gets knocked off balance. If we don't pray, it will stay that way and we have just opened ourselves up for those darts to pass right by the shield and hit us in the breastplate. Then the breastplate gets a few dings in it and before you know it all the other pieces begin to get heavy. We begin to shed pieces to be able to just make it through and we become completely exposed. Satan then comes in and his devouring begins. When we focus our attention on staying armed and in communication then we will be fully prepared and protected.

Steam Cleaned:

Oh Lord, please help me not be another knocked out, knocked down Christian. I don't want to be useless and undone. I want to be a sure and strong weapon in your arsenal. Please remind me to suit up for the battle and remain on guard so that I will be aware and ready when you need to use me. Help me to cover my children and husband as they go to their different places and help them to learn to be aware in their own lives. Thank you for your provision of armor for the spiritual battles we face.

In Jesus Name,

Amen

Dirty Laundry (Personal Evaluation):
Do I walk around unaware? Am I leaving my family unprotected because I refuse to
stay alert to Satan's schemes against us? Am I not prone to spiritual attacks?

Week 3– Day 1 – Mordecai & the Jews

Read Esther Chapter 4

Laundry Basket: Esther 4:1-4
This chapter starts out very dramatic. Mordecai is mourning. Not as we mourn, privately, but very publicly, very loudly. This was and is the way Jews mourn. They would adorn themselves in burlap like clothing and spread ashes all over themselves. Sometimes they would even sit in a pile of ashes. They would wail and cry out loudly. Now in verse 3 it tells us *there was great mourning among the Jews."* It is estimated that 15 million Jews lived in the 127 provinces. There were millions of people in the streets wailing and crying. No one in any of the provinces went unaffected by the news of the day of annihilation of the Jews

Laundry Lesson: I taught my children to sort laundry when they were 5 (Josh) & 4 (Courtney) years old. I purchased 4 clothes baskets: 1-white, 1-blue, 1-red, and 1-green. The children matched the color of the clothes to the color of the basket. All odd colored clothes went into the green basket. We should sort the feelings of mourning that we experience in our lives much like sorting laundry. They each have a specific purpose and any unsorted feelings could be sitting in an unsettled "basket" in our hearts.

Dirty Laundry: Mourning

We mourn over different things. It is not always the death of a loved one. It could be over the loss of a close friendship or major changes in our lives. We mourn over situations that seem unfair. Not all mourning is severe. Some mourning last only a few days, some last years. We also must realize that we can not mourn and those around us be unaffected.

There are several "normal" stages that we must go through to truly mourn completely and healthy:

Denial: This is the stage where you just can't believe it has happened. Most experts agree that this stage is essential so that during the time of great loss we don't lose our minds. Our emotions must adjust so God has built within us a mechanism to help slow down the emotional overload. This stage could be long lived or short and sweet, depends entirely on the individual.

Anger: This is the stage that is exactly what you would think. You are mad at anyone or anything that moves. It could be directly related to the loss or could just be a reaction to anything as a result of the grief. Here again the length of this stage is dependant upon the individual.

Fear: This could also be called the "What if..." stage. This stage is where you begin to feel the affects of the loss and realize the impact it will have on you. This may also be where you feel regret. "If only I had..." This is a normal part of mourning. Fear is associated with this stage in that we are now unsure of the days ahead. This stage is also just a process of time for the individual.

Depression: We hear a lot about depression. It is something that the medical profession has targeted for being associated with several health related issues. It is so important that we allow God to completely heal us of any emotional baggage that may be lingering. Depression can take on many forms. It may cause exhaustion. It may cause you to be anxious. It can be the root of significant weight loss or weight gain. Any and all of these could accompany severe or prolonged depression. Please take note that you do not need to run to your medical doctor as soon as you begin the depression stage of mourning. Most will ride out the storm just fine. Some may need help. If you find yourself unable to adjust seek medical help.

Acceptance: This is the final stage of mourning. Where life begins again and our focus turns from the hurt to the healing. Again, if we suppress our grief process or hinder any part of it we will never find the healing God has in store for us. That healing includes a much more fulfilling relationship with Him. Acceptance does not mean we have arrived, it just means we have come to a place where we are willing to live life with the change and find the memories are sweet instead of painful.

(Remember, after looking through these stages, if you have suffered a great loss and do not remember going through these stages you <u>may</u> have suppressed some of the emotional stuff associated with it. Ask God to help you go back and heal completely.)

List times of mourning that you have experienced:

_____   _____
_____   _____
_____   _____

Laundry Detergent (God's Word): Fill in the blanks.

I Thessalonians 4:13: Brothers, we do not want you to be ignorant about those who _____ _____, or to _____ like the rest of men, who have no _____.

God does not want us to grieve as the world grieves. He has given us a future and a hope.   We need his healing hand to sooth the hurts and pains of mourning.

Steam Cleaned:
For the rest of this lesson spend time with God sorting through the losses of your life and allow God to show you if there are any "baskets" of odd emotions that you have not allowed him to deal with. Use the area below to write any notes that you may have.

<u>Denial:</u>　　What loss:　_____

_____

<u>Anger:</u>　　What loss:　_____

_____

<u>Fear:</u>　　What loss:　_____

_____

<u>Depression:</u> What loss:　_____

_____

Dirty Laundry (Personal Evaluation):
Have I suffered great loss in my life and suppressed feelings? Was I able to sort through loss in my life in a healthy way as a child? Am I completely healthy after seasons of mourning?

Week — Day 2 — Esther

Read Esther Chapter 4

Laundry Basket: Joshua 2:1-19; 6:22-23
Remind us Lord that we all have a part to play, a job to do, a ministry to serve. Help us to seek your will and do our part to see our family and friends find Jesus.

Esther is called to serve. Why would God choose an orphan to change the course of an entire race? Why would God use an ordinary girl to do the job of an extraordinary person? God does because: he completes the weakness so that his strength may shine. God loves to watch those who can't, do!! God is the God who likes to see the underdog win.

Laundry Lesson: Have you ever run the washer without adding laundry detergent? The clothes come out okay but the stains aren't removed. They still have funny smells. It just hasn't done a lot of good to put the clothes in the washer. The washer's job wasn't used to its fullest potential because it wasn't given the proper ingredients. If we live our life without doing our part in the ministry of the Kingdom we are much like the washer without laundry detergent. We will not reach our fullest potential. We will just agitate through life with no purpose or accomplishments to take to heaven with us.

Laundry: Doing Your Part

The linage of Christ is filled with ordinary, even risqué people. His bloodline is not one of Kings and nobles. Not a long history of heroes in the world's eyes. They were ordinary, mistake making people.

Esther is obedient to Mordecai and before the chapter ends Esther has become, in herself, a leader. What a brilliant picture of the kind of strength God gives when he calls you to serve. You cannot imagine the peace that accompanies obedience. You can't believe the joy that fills you when you are working right where God wants you.

Also, God has not given you an assignment for just your own fulfillment. What God asks you to do is not only for your good and his glory; it is for the good of everyone. This means, not only is he calling you and desires for you to be where he wants you, you have responsibilities to everyone else to do what God has called you to do. What would have happened if Rehab, Esther, Saul and most importantly Jesus had refused to answer the call? *We would all be sinners bound for an eternal Hell.* Could it be that because you have not answered

God's call that someone in your life is unsaved? We need to take seriously the leading of the Holy Spirit in our lives. It could mean the difference of salvation or destruction to someone around us.

Esther when she is called to serve is first timid and unsure. She doesn't believe she can do it. She even refuses at first. Then when she realizes the impact of the tiny word "NO," she surrenders. What about you? Have you answered the call that God has for you? Are you waiting for someone else to volunteer? God can use anything or anybody, but he chose YOU.

What areas am I currently following God's direction of serving:

_____   _____
_____   _____
_____   _____

Laundry Detergent (God's Word): Fill in the blanks.

I Corinthians 12:7:   Now to _____ one the manifestation of the _____ is given for the _____ _____.

I Corinthians 12:18: But in fact _____ has arranged the parts in the body, every one of them, _____ ____ _____ _____ them to be.

Make notes about the things you are to do in the family of God:
- _____
- _____
- _____

Steam Cleaned:
Lord, how I want to take my place in the body of Christ. Please help me to know where and what my responsibilities are. Help me know when to say no and when to step in and help. Please direct my steps to help see people come to know you as Savior.

In Jesus Name,
Amen

Dirty Laundry (Personal Evaluation):
What is God's call on my life? Am I listening when God speaks? Do I see God's hand of direction on my life?

Week 3 — Day 3 — Maids & Chamberlains

Read Esther Chapter 4

Laundry Basket: Esther 4:1-4

Let's consider Esther's maids and chamberlains. These were men and women appointed to serve the queen. Those who served the queen must have loved her very much. They were not required to tell her about Mordecai mourning in the gate. They did not have to pay attention to the queen and her relatives but they did. They took interest in things that would affect the queen. They cared about Esther, not just because she was queen but because she was their friend. Look at verse 16: *I and my maids will fast as you do.* Imagine Esther asking her maids to take such actions if they were not close friends.

Laundry Lesson: It's a cold winter morning. Out the door you go. You look down - Static cling. You shake, you twist, and you pull and tug. Still there! That's how friends should be in our lives. We should have friends that love us and stick with us through all situations and mood swings.

Laundry: Friends

Friendship is a wonderful gift God has given us. We need friends. We need relationships. God designed us that way. We are to be and have friends. Let's discover what God calls a friend and what we are to do to be good friends as these maid and chamberlains were to Esther.

Friends are sometimes called to say the hard things. Friends should share everything and love each other unconditionally, the hurts and the joys.

We all need different types of friends in our lives. Below is a chart with the different types and the explanation of each type. Fill the chart with the friends in your life. If you don't have a friend to list in a category leave it blank. Some friends may fit into more than one category.

Type	Explanation	Name of Friend
Admonisher	Warns when you're heading off track	
Celebrator	Believes in you and applauds your successes	
Encourager	Strengthens your spirit	
Intercessor	Prays for you/ Spiritual warfare for you	
Mentor	Those who can share wisdom with you	
Planner	Those who help with decision making	
Counselor	Advises and assists through struggles	

From Judith Couchman's book *Esther*.

What type friends, from the list above, do I not want around me and why:

_____   _____
_____   _____
_____   _____

Laundry Detergent (God's word): Fill in the blanks.

Friend in the following verses mean: brother, companion, neighbor.

Job 16:21: on _____ of a man he pleads with God, as a man _____ for his _____.

Proverbs 17:17: A _____ loves at _____ _____, and a brother is born for adversity.

Proverbs 27:6: Wounds from a _____ can be trusted, but an _____ multiplies kisses.

Proverbs 27:9: Perfume and incense bring joy to the heart, and the pleasantness of one's _____ springs from his _____ _____.

Specific steps I need to take to gain different types of friends:
- _____
- _____
- _____

Steam Cleaned:

Lord, help me be responsive to different kinds of people that you bring into my life to teach me more about myself and you. Help me to be open to new types of friendships to help me be a more healthy and productive Christian. Cause me to be a healthy friend to those in my life.

In Jesus name,

Amen

Dirty Laundry (Personal Evaluation):
Do I shut myself off from people who could fill a "friend" spot in my life? Do I need to be friendlier to allow God to bring women into my life to help fill in the friend spots that I am lacking?

Week 3 — Day 4 — Jews

Read Esther Chapter 4

Laundry Basket: Esther 4:16

God called Esther to stand in the gap for the Jews, but he also needed the Jews to stand in the gap for Esther. They were to support the work that Esther was to do. They were to be the silent partners, if you will. The mission needed everyone to do their part for it to succeed.

Laundry Lesson: I remember when I didn't have a washer and dryer and had to go to the Laundromat. I would load the washers and then wait. When the washers finish I would find a laundry cart to carry the load from the washers to the dryers. Without the cart the job is extremely difficult and heavy. That is how the family of God is when we all do our part. The job is easy and light when we are doing our part. When someone is not doing their part to stand in the gap we all suffer.

Laundry: Standing in the Gap

As members of the body of Christ and a local church we have a job to do also. The ministry of the church can not be fulfilled without everyone being silent partners. We are the staff's support system. The ministry of the Pastor is not to do all the visiting and witnessing, that is our job. The pastor's job is to prepare us for the work. The church, its classes, and services are to prepare us for the witnessing we should do in our daily lives. We are called to be the prayer support and the mission support team of the church. We are to pray <u>daily</u> for the ministries and staff of the church. We are to seek God's face on behalf of the church.

What are the hindrances that cause me not to do my part:

_____   _____
_____   _____
_____   _____

Laundry Detergent (God's Word): Fill in the blanks.

I Corinthians 3:9-10 for we are God's _____ workers; you are God's field, God's _____. By the grace God has given me, I laid a foundation as an expert builder, and someone else is building on it. But each one should be _____ how he builds.

Paul's message was to work together to accomplish a greater good. It is Christ's church and he is the foundation.

Below is a list of areas that we should be praying for on a regular basis for our church and its staff. Include notes for each area listed for specific requests that you know of that would be something you could begin to pray for during you quiet time.

Steam Cleaned:

Pastor:

Other Ministers:

Support Staff:

Deacons:

Senior Adult Ministry:

Adult Ministry:

Youth Ministry:

Children's Ministry:

Preschool Ministry:

Prayer Ministry:

Worship Ministry:

Other Ministries:

As the time of Christ's return draws closer it becomes more important that we pray for our church and those in leadership. Begin now to take you place on the team of praying for your church family.

Dirty Laundry (Personal Evaluation):
Am I standing in the gap for my local church? Do I pray daily for the staff and ministries of my church? Can the family of God depend on me?

Week 3 — Day 5 — Esther
Read Esther Chapter 5

Laundry Basket: Esther 5:1-4
Verse 2 says *when the King saw Esther standing in the court, she obtained favor in his sight."*

The word "obtained" there means - pardon, regard, respect. Favor takes on the meaning – grace, pleasant and precious.

Laundry Lesson: Ever put a new red shirt in the wash with a load of whites. Everything turns pink. The red from the new shirt covers the color of the other garments. The white clothes now have the color content of the red garment. That is the same principle with God and our acceptance. When Jesus becomes our Savior his "content" becomes ours and he "fades" on us. We now have Jesus' content that means we have God's content, which makes us acceptable.

Laundry: Acceptance

Esther received grace from the King. She was given something that she did not deserve or could even ask for. She was given acceptance. What a beautiful picture of Christ's love that he lavishes on us when he extends his salvation to us.

Things that work against my believing in the acceptance of God in my life:

_____	_____
_____	_____
_____	_____

Laundry Detergent (God's Word): Fill in the blanks.

Romans 8:15 For you did not receive a spirit that makes you a _____ again to fear, but you received the Spirit of _____ And by him we cry, _____.

Galatians 4:5 to _____ those under law, that we might receive the full _____ of _____.

58

Ephesians 1:5 he _____ us to be _____ as his _____ through Jesus Christ, in accordance with his _____ and will...

It is wonderful that God chose to use the term adoption for those of us in Christ Jesus. Even in our day and age adoption is a very serious thing. Something a lot of people do not realize about adoption is the fact that as an adoptive parent you can not change your mind about the child. I, as a biological parent can drop my children at the door of a hospital and disown them. But, if I adopt a child, I can never turn my back on that adopted child. The law requires me to be the mother of that child forever. Whether the child grows up to be president or a mass murderer, I have to claim him as my child. Isn't that great that God used that; He knew that some of us hard headed people would need a concrete perspective on salvation so that we would not question our security. Once we accept Jesus as our Savior, we are adopted into the family. That means we are a member of the family.

Romans 8:17 Now if we are _____, then we are heirs—heirs of God and _____ with Christ, if indeed we share in his sufferings in order that we may also _____ in his _____.

Titus 3:7 so that, having been _____ by his grace, we might become _____ having the hope of _____ _____.

As joint heirs with Christ, that gives us access to the riches of Heaven; the most important of those riches being access to God the Father. We are heirs to the throne; that means we <u>have</u> to be children of God. Just like here on earth, children of an earthly King or Queen are heirs to the throne. They inherit what the parents have. Wow, what a thought. We inherit, face to face time with Jesus, Heaven and eternal life.

Look again at Romans 8:15, it talks about us receiving the "Spirit of Sonship" (KJV calls it adoption). This is talking about the Holy Spirit. So to say that we have received the spirit of adoption is like having the court rule for the adoptive parents and everything becoming legal and binding for the adoptive parents. Once the papers are signed and the court has ruled, the adoption is sealed and can not be reversed by the adoptive parent. Now because the Holy Spirit is our binding agreement with God our hearts cry out "daddy" to God the father.

When you adopt a child that child now <u>can</u> call you mommy. This is what God is pointing out. He is now our father, daddy. We are now free to know him so intimately that we would cry out for our daddy. Talk about acceptance. We have been placed in a royal linage. We too have been orphaned (unsaved) and now are royalty. My how our lives should be different.

Acceptance is something that we long for. The need to be loved and accepted is part of our nature. But to search for acceptance in the people of this earth will only lead to disappointment. People do not love unconditionally, their acceptance changes, sometimes daily. With God, acceptance is forever. We are accepted because of what Jesus did for us. We always have access to God, we are always royalty, and we are always daughters of the King.

3 verses to memorize to assure you of your acceptance in Christ:
- --
- --
- --

Steam Cleaned:

Lord, please help me find my acceptance in you. Help me know that you find me precious. How I need to know in the deepest parts of my heart that you fully love and want me. Thank you for letting me be a part of the family. Thank you that my name is always on your mind. You truly are my light and salvation.

In Jesus Name,

Amen

Dirty Laundry (Personal Evaluation):
Do I truly believe I am precious to God? Do I believe I am fully and completely accepted? Do I believe that I have found favor with God?

Week 4 — Day 1 — Haman

Read Esther Chapter 5

Laundry Lesson: A stain stick is something you use when you need control over a stain in a specific area. It allows you to apply cleaning solution directly to a stained portion of a garment. Self-Control is like a stain stick. It needs to be applied specifically to areas of our lives that would not bring God honor.

Laundry: Self-Control

Laundry Basket: Esther 5:9-11 *Haman went out that day happy and in high spirits. But when he saw Mordecai at the king's gate and observed that he neither rose nor showed fear in his presence, he was filled with rage against Mordecai. ¹⁰ Nevertheless, Haman restrained himself and went home. Calling together his friends and Zeresh, his wife, ¹¹ Haman boasted to them about his vast wealth, his many sons, and all the ways the king had honored him and how he had elevated him above the other nobles and officials.*

The word "restrained" in verse 10 means: contain, abstain, force oneself to restrain. So Haman has to use self-control to keep himself from attacking Mordecai. Funny, Haman can control himself when he knows that others are watching and it would make him look bad to act upon his anger. But deep inside he is filled with hatred because Mordecai will not worship him. He makes a conscience effort to control himself against Mordecai. Haman chooses a character trait that we as Christians should exhibit regularly. We have the power of the Holy Spirit within us to help us "restrain" ourselves from acting like unbelievers.

List areas of your life lacking self-control:

_____ _____
_____ _____
_____ _____

Laundry Detergent (God's Word): Fill in the blanks.

Galatians 5:22-23 But the fruit of the Spirit is love, joy, peace, _____, kindness, goodness, faithfulness, ²³gentleness and _____. Against such things there is no law.
Self-control, temperance means simple to control oneself. If only we could do this. Be careful to notice that Self-control is one of the outward signs of the

fruit of the spirit. This means when we are living a spirit controlled life that we will exhibit these attributes.

Love – for God and others

Joy – assurance of salvation; assurance of right standing with God

Peace – Calmness of Spirit

Patience – Longsuffering, Endurance

Kindness – moral excellence

Goodness – virtue

Faithfulness – belief, constancy in profession

Gentleness – meekness, humility

Self-control – temperance

II Peter 1:5-11 [5]For this very reason, make every effort to add to your faith goodness; and to goodness, knowledge; [6]and to knowledge, _____; and to self-control, _____; and to perseverance, _____; [7]and to godliness, brotherly kindness; and to brotherly kindness, love. [8]For if you possess these qualities in increasing measure, they will keep you from being _____ and _____ in your knowledge of our Lord Jesus Christ. [9]But if anyone does not have them, he is _____ and _____, and has _____ that he has been cleansed from his past sins. [10]Therefore, my brothers, be all the more eager to make your calling and election sure. For if you do these things, you will never fall, [11]and you will receive a rich welcome into the eternal kingdom of our Lord and Savior Jesus Christ

Notice verse 8 tells us that if we are to add goodness, knowledge, self-control, perseverance, godliness, brotherly kindness and love to our spirit filled life we will not be ineffective and unproductive in our knowledge of Jesus. It would be like saying we are unemployed Christians; Lazy, useless or idle Christians. That's what the meanings of the words ineffective and unproductive means. Oh, how we need to live a spirit controlled life.

Verse 9 states that when we do not add to our spiritual life these things we are nearsighted and blind. These words bring the meaning of not being able to see clearly the reality of the cleansing and reality of the Holy Spirit in our lives. We have not worked to become the godly model that we profess. We <u>choose</u> to lay down our desires and fleshly cravings and <u>choose</u> to live a life controlled by the spirit. It's not easy to realize that we choose to live a life of ungodliness. It doesn't sit well to find that we can live with all the attributes by making a choice.

3 steps to adding self-control to my daily life:

- _____
- _____
- _____

Steam Cleaned:

Lord, help me choose godliness. Help me to lay down my wants and desires and submit to your spirit's control. How I want self-control to be the normal pattern of my life and I realize that without the spirit's guidance that is impossible. Please help me to choose you each day so that my life will be a living testimony for you.

In Jesus Name,

Amen

Dirty Laundry (Personal Evaluation):
Am I keeping my attitude and actions in check with God's directions? Is a spirit-filled
life the normal pattern of my life?

Week 4 — Day 2 — King Xerxes

Read Esther Chapter 6

Laundry Lesson: Ever watched the agitator inside the washer. It moves side to side, up and down, twisting and turning the clothes. It looks as if it is having a fit. It reminds me of restlessness. No sleep, unable to relax, nothing seems comfortable. Restlessness, it can be miserable.

Dirty Laundry: Restlessness

Laundry Basket: Esther 6:1

That night the king could not sleep; so he ordered the book of the chronicles, the record of his reign, to be brought in and read to him.

God's divine hand is all over the king at this point. King Xerxes is restless. Sleep will not come to the King. Sometimes our restlessness is brought about by God. Other times it is brought on by our own doing. In King Xerxes case it is obviously the intervening of God. God wants the king to be aware of an oversight.

I have found those middle of the night times with God to be some of the most precious times I have spent with him. Sometimes it was just to cause me to pray for someone. Sometimes it was to deal with some deep rooted sin in my life. Either way to have God to wake you to spend time with him is a great blessing.

The next time sleep won't come, don't reach for the sleeping pills, maybe God needs to spend some quality time with you. You see, when God causes us to be restless it is because he is moving and doesn't want us to miss it.

Let's look at restlessness brought about by worry or anxiety. This is not a working of God. We work this up in our minds and begin the mental treadmill. "What if...?", "How can I...?", "Maybe I should...?"

Laundry Detergent (God's Word): Fill in the blanks.

Luke 10:41 Martha, Martha," the Lord answered, "you are _____ and _____ about many things.

66

List the things you worry over:

_____   _____
_____   _____
_____   _____

Luke 12:29 And do not _____ _____ _____ on what you will eat or drink; do not _____ about it.

I Peter 5:7 Cast all your _____ on him because he cares for you.

We have all read or heard these verses many times. When we will take them to heart and make them part of the truth that changes our lives.

Matthew 6:25-33 Therefore I tell you, do not _____ about your life, what you will _____ or _____; or about your body, what you will _____. Is not life more important than food, and the body more important than clothes? [26]Look at the birds of the air; they do not _____ or _____ or _____ away in barns, and yet your heavenly Father feeds them. Are you not _____ _____ _____ than they? [27]Who of you by _____can add a single hour to his life? [28]"And why do you _____ about _____? See how the lilies of the field grow. They do not labor or spin. [29]Yet I tell you that not even Solomon in all his splendor was dressed like one of these. [30]If that is how God clothes the grass of the field, which is here today and tomorrow is thrown into the fire, will he not much more clothe you, O you of little faith? [31]So do not _____, saying, 'What shall we eat?' or 'What shall we drink?' or 'What shall we wear?' [32]For the pagans run after all these things and your heavenly Father knows that you need them. [33]But seek _____ his kingdom and his righteousness, and all these things will be given to you as well.

List 3 things you will give to Jesus today that you will no longer worry over:

- _____
- _____
- _____

Steam Cleaned:

Oh Lord, help me to hide the truth of your word in the depths of my heart. Help me to put worry and restlessness away so that I may concentrate on you and your intentions. Help me be sure of your provision for my family and make me strongly aware of your presence in situations that cause me to want to worry and fret. Help me rely on you for my help and strength and not to look to the things of the world for security.

In Jesus Name,

Amen

Dirty Laundry (Personal Evaluation):
Do I spend countless hours worrying or restless? Am I unable to relax? Do I have more than 2 sleepless nights a week?

Week 4 — Day 3 — Mordecai

Read Esther Chapter 6

Laundry Basket: Esther 6:11-13

So Haman got the robe and the horse. He robed Mordecai, and led him on horseback through the city streets, proclaiming before him, "This is what is done for the man the king delights to honor!" 12 Afterward Mordecai returned to the king's gate. But Haman rushed home, with his head covered in grief, 13 and told Zeresh his wife and all his friends everything that had happened to him.

Laundry Lesson: Ever take time to notice the difference between a load of laundry from the dryer with a fabric softener and one without a fabric softener sheet. The one without the fabric softener sheet pops and snaps and makes all sorts of noises. The load with the fabric softener sheet is soft and quiet. Our lives are like this. When we are spirit controlled we learn to close our mouths instead of "snap & pop" off at every little thing.

Laundry: Tamed Tongue

Notice, the whole time God was teaching Haman a valuable lesson, Mordecai was silent. He did not let his words ruin what God was doing. He understood that this was a time to keep silent. Mordecai understood there was a greater purpose working than the humiliation of Haman. Though with earthly eyes, Mordecai had every right to say "I told you so," Mordecai chose to remain silent. While Haman was carrying him through the streets, Mordecai did not speak. He did not add to Haman's shame.

Have you ever noticed that it is easy to realize you shouldn't say something, after you've said it? The virtue of silence is the ability to determine when to speak and when to hold your tongue.

List times you wished you had remained silent:

_____   _____

_____   _____

_____   _____

Laundry Detergent (God's Word): Fill in the blanks.

Ecclesiastes 3:1-8 There is a time for everything, and a season for every activity under heaven: a time to be born and a time to die, a time to plant and a time to uproot, a time to kill and a time to heal, a time to tear down and a time to build, a time to weep and a time to laugh, a time to mourn and a time to dance, a time to scatter stones and a time to gather them, a time to embrace and a time to refrain, a time to search and a time to give up, a time to keep and a time to throw away, a time to tear and a time to mend, a time to be _____ and a time to _____, a time to love and a time to hate, a time for war and a time for peace.

Proverbs 17:28 Even a fool is thought wise if he keeps _____, and _____ if he holds his tongue.

Proverbs 18:7 A fool's _____ is his undoing, and his _____ are a snare to his soul.

Proverbs 29:11 A fool gives _____ _____ to his anger, but a wise man keeps himself _____ _____.

Proverbs 29:20 Do you see a man who _____ in haste? There is more hope for a _____ than for him.

Ecclesiastes 5:3 As a dream comes when there are many _____, so the _____of a fool when there are many _____.

Ecclesiastes 10:12 _____ from a wise man's mouth are _____, but a _____ is consumed by his _____ _____.

Interesting: When the bible talks about someone who cannot hold their tongue it calls them a "fool." Fool means: stupid or silly. God doesn't want his children to be fools. He wants us to live holy lives; Controlled by the spirit; So that we don't open our mouths and make ourselves and Him a fool. How many times have we opened our mouths and then wished with everything within us that we had remained silent.

Steam Cleaned:
Dear Lord, Help me learn to live a life completely controlled by you; One that my words honor you; a life that turn others to you and not away from you. Help me be an example by living a life of holding my tongue when others would speak; living a life that would use words to speak life to those around me and not words that would speak destruction. Help me honor you with my words.

In Jesus Name,
Amen

Dirty Laundry (Personal Evaluation):
Do I speak before I think? Do I ever remain silent when I should? Is my tongue
controlled by the spirit? Can God depend on me to keep silent when needed?

Week 4 — Day 4 — Mordecai
Read Esther Chapter 6

Laundry Basket:
Esther 6:11-12 *So Haman got the robe and the horse. He robed Mordecai, and led him on horseback through the city streets, proclaiming before him, "This is what is done for the man the king delights to honor!" Afterward Mordecai returned to the king's gate. But Haman rushed home, with his head covered in grief*

What did Mordecai do after the parade was finished?

_____

Laundry Lesson: There is nothing like the feeling of a nice warm, cozy towel fresh from the dryer. So inviting. So comforting. So relaxing. That's exactly how life is when we are finding our satisfaction in Jesus, when nothing else will do.

Laundry: Contentment

You see, Mordecai knew where his true contentment lay. Not in some vain honoring from the King. His contentment came from the Lord, so that when changes came he did not get puffed up. He knew his standing with the Father and was satisfied. Mordecai was not looking to make a name for himself. He was not to proud to go back to life as usual after something of great magnitude had happened. He knew his place with God and was content where God had him.

List areas that cause you to struggle with contentment:

_____   _____
_____   _____
_____   _____

Laundry Detergent (God's Word): Fill in the blanks.
Philippians 4:11 I am not saying this because I am in need, for I have _____ to be _____ whatever the _____.
> (Make note that the verse here shows that contentment is learned and that it is in spite of circumstances.)

Hebrews 13:5 [5]Keep your lives free from the _____ _____ _____ and be _____ with what you have, because God has said, "Never will I leave you; never will I forsake you

I Timothy 6:6-8 But _____ with _____ is great gain. [7]For we brought _____ into the world, and we can take nothing out of it. But if we have food and clothing, we will be _____ with that.

Psalm 17:15 And I—in righteousness I will see your face; when I awake, I will be _____ with seeing your likeness.

Psalm 90:14 _____ us in the morning with your unfailing love that we may sing for joy and be glad all our days.

God wants us to be satisfied with him and nothing or no one else. We are to find complete contentment in him and him only.

Commit 3 areas of your life to Jesus to learn contentment through trusting God to satisfy the desire:
- _____
- _____
- _____

Steam Cleaned:
Lord, help me to spend time with you that would cause me to learn contentment in you and only you. I realize that I can not learn contentment without time spent in your presence learning about you. Please help me to hunger and thirst after you so that my desires and satisfactions only find their rest in you.
In Jesus Name,
Amen

Dirty Laundry (Personal Evaluation):
Am I content with where God has me today? Am I content with the "things" I have?
Do I find my contentment in Jesus or in other things?

Week 4 — Day 5 — Mordecai

Read Esther Chapter 6

Laundry Basket: Esther 6:7-9

Mordecai was to wear the King's royal robes. He was to dress as if he were the King. But Mordecai is just a commoner. Now in a moment's time he is dressed in royal apparel. The most humble of men, exalted to the fullest. The most unlikely, wearing the clothing of the King.

Laundry Lesson: Ever picked up your dry-cleaning, get it home and discover you have someone else's clothes. Nicer than yours. It would be so awesome if that beautiful gown was yours? You would be the talk of the town if you were to be seen in that dress. But it doesn't belong to you. It belongs to someone more important. That's how it is going to be when we wear Christ's royal robes in heaven. We don't deserve to wear them but what an exciting time.

Laundry: Robed in Royalty

There is another place in scripture where common clothes were exchanged for royal apparel. Read I Samuel 18:1-4

Jonathan loved David so much he was willing to trade his royalty for David's poverty. What a wonderful picture this paints. Jesus traded his glory and splendor for a garment of flesh so that we could wear royal attire.

Let's look at one other place in scripture where someone undeserving receives the finest of apparel. Read Luke 15:11-27.

In all three cases, Mordecai, David and the prodigal son, each one received clothing that was of higher value than they could attain themselves. Each time the clothing represented great value or worth. These men were treated with worth.

List times you have been treated special:

_____   _____
_____   _____
_____   _____

Laundry Detergent (God's Word): Fill in the blanks.

Revelation 19:7-8 let us rejoice and be glad and give him glory! For the wedding of the Lamb has come, and his bride has made herself ready. Fine _____, _____ and _____ was given her to wear." (Fine linen stands for the righteous acts of the saints.)

Once we receive Christ, anything we do for Christ will be woven into a royal wedding gown. We will be given garments fit for a Queen and that is only through the washing away of our sins through the blood of Jesus Christ, and our walking daily in his ways.

Remember the hymn:
        I dare not trust the sweetest frame but holy lean on Jesus name.
             Dressed in his righteousness alone
            Faultless to stand before the throne.

              On Christ the solid rock I stand
              All other ground is sinking sand
              All other ground is sinking sand

How amazing that day will be, when we stand before God, unworthy, but justified, dressed in royal apparel, never to be mistaken for a commoner again.

List 3 things you are anticipating about your royal wedding:
- _____
- _____
- _____

Steam Cleaned:
Lord, please help me understand the awesome time that awaits me as a child of yours. May I begin to live my life as an offering of thanksgiving to you for the gift of forgiveness? I can't wait to see you face to face and I pray my life would be one that would bring pleasure to you as you watch me live to glorify you.
Amen

Dirty Laundry (Personal Evaluation):
Am I sure of my royal robe waiting for me? Am I anticipating the time when dressed
in royal robes I will be in heaven with Jesus?

Week 5 — Day 1 — Esther

Read Esther Chapter 7

Laundry Lesson: I love to hang sheets outside on a clothes line to dry. They smell so good and are so comfortable. They are fresh and clean. So are words rightly chosen and softly spoken. Only God can give those words. Only God can make hard words soft or confronting words gracious.

Laundry: Gracious Words

Laundry Basket:

Proverbs 15:1 *A gentle answer turns away wrath, but a harsh word stirs up anger.*

Proverbs 16:24 *Pleasant words are a honeycomb, sweet to the soul and healing to the bones.*

These are the kind of words that Esther used. She knew she had to speak as not to bring wrath upon herself or her people. She also realized that the choosing of her words could also seem that she was condemning the King also. Remember he is the one who gave Haman permission to issue the decree. Esther's word had to be bathed in prayer. If she had gone in and with wrathful words, blaming everyone she could have caused a great harm. But instead she waited. She planned. She prayed and then she dripped honey on the soul of the King. Esther knew the value of soft, pleasant words. She was a woman who knew how to choose her words. How differently chapter 7 would have ended if Esther's words had not been aptly chosen. How godly Esther must have been. To be in such a crucial point and have the poise and control that she exhibited shows great character.

List times in your life when soft words would have turned away wrath:

---------------------   ---------------------
---------------------   ---------------------
---------------------   ---------------------

Laundry Detergent (God's Word): Fill in the blanks.

Colossians 4:6 Let your _____ be always full of grace, seasoned with _____, so that you may know how to _____ everyone.

Proverbs 25:11 A _____ aptly spoken is like apples of _____ in settings of silver.

Aptly means to revolve. Like the spoke of a wheel that fits perfectly and makes the wheel turn smoothly.

Soft words, pleasant words, apt words are those that we should use. Words that are covered in godly influence and spiced with moral insight should be a regular occurrence in our lives. Conversation should be sweetness to the soul of the one receiving the words.

How our Father wants our conversation to be that of richness and soft words. We are to model godly character and speech in our lives. Who knows what sweet words might draw a man to Christ.

List 3 steps to take to temper your words by God's grace:
- _____
- _____
- _____

Steam Cleaned:

Dear Father, how I want to be a woman of soft words. I want to drip honey from my lips. I want to speak the truth in love. Please help me to choose words spiced with prudence. Let my speech be filled with divine influence. Us my tongue to speak honey to the soul of others; May the words I use show forth fruit of worth. Help me to become a woman that when I speak others find honor and great spiritual wealth. Train my lips to honor you in everything I say. "Let the words of my mouth and the meditation of my heart be acceptable in thy sight, O Lord my strength and my redeemer."

In Jesus Name,

Amen

Dirty Laundry (Personal Evaluation):
Do I ask God to temper my words with grace? Do I speak rashly or harshly? Are my words soft, gracious words?

Week 5 — Day 2 — Haman
Read Esther Chapter 7

Laundry Basket: Esther 7:8-10
Haman's plan has just blown up in his face. He is sitting before the King and the entire city is aware of the gallows in his front yard. Gallows meant for Mordecai. Now he sits with his face covered totally devastated; Haman has been put to shame. The covering of the face was a sign of shame. No one could view his face because he had brought shame upon himself. His destructive desires have now caused his own shame and downfall. How quickly he found that evil did not pay. Remember, this is the evening after Mordecai had been honored, and it is only a few days since the decree to destroy the Jews was issued. He reaped the consequences quickly. He was completely shamed and humiliated.

Laundry Lesson: Mustard stains easily. It spreads and leaves a big mess. Mustard is hard if not impossible to remove; so to is shame. Shame can smear our family name. It can leave a big mess and is next to impossible to remove humanly.

Dirty Laundry: Shame

Haman's shame will eventually fall on his entire family. What an awful heritage to give to his children.

List some times you have experienced shame:

_____   _____
_____   _____
_____   _____

Laundry Detergent (God's Word): Fill in the blanks.

Proverbs 3:35 the wise inherit _____, but fools he holds up to _____.

Proverbs 11:2 When _____ comes, then comes _____, but with _____comes wisdom.

What then would be the opposite of shame and what do we do to have it?

Proverbs 13:5 the righteous hate what is false, but the wicked bring _____ and _____.

Hate here means: to be offensive morally or to stink. With this definition what does this verse teach us? _____

Proverbs 14:35 king delights in a wise servant, but a _____ servant incurs his wrath.

Let me write this verse with the definitions included: *The King's grace, delight or pleasure is toward an expert, prudent, skillful or understanding servant: but his outburst of passion, anger or rage is against him that causes disappointment.*   This is what Haman has experienced.

Proverbs 18:13 He who answers before _____ —that is his folly and his _____.

Proverbs 29:15 the rod of _____ imparts wisdom, but a child left to himself _____ his mother.

Did you notice that each of these actions that brought about shame was brought about by the one who receives the shame? There is no shame put on us by others that is legitimate. Shame comes when we bring it upon ourselves. We would be wise to heed the words of God so as not to bring shame upon ourselves and our family.

From the verses above list 3 steps to preventing shame in your life:

- _____
- _____
- _____

Steam Cleaned:

Lord, help me to live in such a way as not to bring shame upon myself or my family. May my life be one free of shame and disgrace. Please reveal to me areas where I am treading dangerously close to the "shame" boundary and help me to run from it.

In Jesus Name,

Amen

Dirty Laundry (Personal Evaluation):

Do I ensnare myself in shame? Do I cause my family shame? Do I live a shameful existence? Do I live a careless life that would allow shame?

Week 5 — Day 3 — Mordecai

Read Esther Chapter 7

Laundry Basket: Esther 7
Notice in Chapter 7 that Mordecai was defended and he was nowhere around. How many times do we feel we have to be part of our own defense?

Laundry Lesson: Scotchguard, greatest invention ever made if you apply if ahead of time. If you don't some clothing could be ruined in the rain. But if the scotchguard is present you don't even have to think about it. That's how God's defense for us is. It is sure and true!!! God will always defend the righteous, his word promises.

Laundry: Our defense

Mordecai was only mentioned in this Chapter in reference to the gallows that stood in Haman's yard. Yet, his life was defended and the revenge God took did not include Mordecai at all. How many times has God been ready to be our defender and we have stepped in to help God (without his leading). God was fully prepared to save Mordecai's life. God fully intended to defend Mordecai. He fully intended to right the wrong done against his chosen.

List areas that you are trying to defend yourself:

_____   _____
_____   _____
_____   _____

Laundry Detergent (God's Word): Fill in the blanks.

God is our _____ and strength, an ever-present _____ in trouble. Therefore we will not fear, though the earth _____ _____ and the _____ _____ into the heart of the sea, though is waters roar and foam and the mountains quake with their surging. Selah. There is a river whose streams make glad the city of God, the holy place where the Most High dwells. God is within her, she will not fall; God will help her at break of day. Nations are in uproar, kingdoms fall; he lifts his voice, the earth melts. The LORD Almighty is _____ us; the God of Jacob is our _____. Selah. Come and see the works of the LORD, the desolations he has brought on the earth. He makes wars cease to the ends of the earth; he breaks the bow and shatters the spear, he burns the shields with fire. "Be still, and know that I am God; I will be exalted among the nations, I will be exalted in the earth." The LORD Almighty is with us; the God of Jacob is our _____.

Psalm 59:9 O my _____, I watch for you; you, O God, are my _____.

Psalm 59:16 But I will sing of your _____, in the morning I will sing of your love; for you are my _____, my _____ in times of trouble.

Psalm 62:6-7 He alone is my _____ and my _____; he is my _____, I will not be shaken. My salvation and my honor depend on God he is my mighty_____, my _____.

Psalm 91:2 I will say of the LORD, "He is my _____ and my _____, my God, in whom I trust."

Psalm 94:22 But the LORD has become my _____, and my God the _____ in whom I take _____.

Refuge means: shelter, hope, a place of trust, defense, high fort or cliff. Defense means: inaccessible place or high fort.

So, if God is our cliff or inaccessible place that means that we are safe; that our defense is sure. Who do you know that could undo anything that God does? God is our defense. Have you ever taken time to consider that? God is our protection. Is there anyone better fit for the job. God Almighty, Superman of all Supermen, Great and Mighty Tower, he is our defense. He not only takes on the job of daddy when we receive Christ but he takes on our enemies also.

List 3 areas that you will give to God today and allow him to be your defense:
- _____
- _____
- _____

Steam Cleaned:

Lord, please help me to allow you to be my defense. Remind me not to get in your way as you defend me. Help me rest in you and the fact that you will make right those things done against me. Help me to realize that as my father you take personally the acts done against me to cause me harm. Help me to believe that you are my refuge and strength and rest in that fully. In Jesus Name, Amen

Dirty Laundry (Personal Evaluation):
Do I trust God to defend me? Am I looking for ways to defend myself? Am I completely convinced that God will make right the wrongs done against me?

Week 5 — Day 4 — Mordecai

Read Esther Chapter 8

Laundry Basket: As we have discovered, Mordecai's patience has been rewarded indeed. For Mordecai, waiting for a reward was not an unbearable task, why, because he didn't expect one. He realized his worth outside of Christ and knew he didn't deserve anything. He knew salvation itself was reward enough. Every indication says that Mordecai did what was right because he was an obedient servant. When the reward was received he was truly grateful.

Laundry Lesson: Do you get as excited as I do when I open the washer or dryer to find a dollar has been left in a pocket? It is understood in our home that what I find in the pockets, good or bad, is mine. What an unexplained surprise. This is how our rewards should be with God; always unexpected, completed humbling and always undeserved.

Laundry: Rewards

Read again Mordecai's actions that are now being rewarded:

Esther 2:21-23 *During the time Mordecai was sitting at the king's gate, Bigthana and Teresh, two of the king's officers who guarded the doorway, became angry and conspired to assassinate King Xerxes. But Mordecai found out about the plot and told Queen Esther, who in turn reported it to the king, giving credit to Mordecai. And when the report was investigated and found to be true, the two officials were hanged on a gallows. All this was recorded in the book of the annals in the presence of the king.*

Three verses written about the actions of Mordecai; look at the list of rewards he received. After each scripture reference list the reward he was given:

Esther 6:8-10: _____
Esther 8:2: _____
Esther 8:7-8 _____
Esther 8:15-17 _____

List rewards you are expecting:

_____   _____
_____   _____
_____   _____

Laundry Detergent (God's Word): Fill in the blanks.

Ruth 2:12 May the LORD _____ you for what you have done. May you be richly _____ by the LORD, the God of Israel, under whose wings you have come to take refuge."

Psalm 58:11 Then men will say, "_____ the righteous still are _____; surely there is a God who judges the earth."

Proverbs 11:18 The wicked man earns _____ _____, but he who sows righteousness reaps a _____ _____.

Proverbs 22:4 Humility and the fear of the LORD bring wealth and _____ and _____.

Matthew 16:27 For the Son of Man is going to come in his Father's glory with his angels, and then he will _____ each person according to what he has _____.

Luke 6:35 But love your enemies, do good to them, and lend to them without expecting to get anything back. Then your _____ will be _____, and you will be sons of the Most High, because he is kind to the ungrateful and wicked.

I Corinthians 3:8 the man who plants and the man who waters have _____ _____, and each will be _____ according to his own labor.

These verses tell us that we will receive a reward, but none of them tell us to look for or expect a reward. Some rewards are reserved for heaven. God is faithful and his word does promise rewards. We will spend many wasted hours looking for rewards when we could be using those moments to bring even more to the throne room of God.

What should I focus my attention on instead of the reward:

- _____
- _____
- _____

Steam Cleaned:

Lord, help me be satisfied with you as my reward. Help me to focus on the work of the kingdom like Mordecai did and not on the reward. Forgive me for wasting time expecting to be rewarded.

In Jesus Name, Amen

Dirty Laundry (Personal Evaluation):
Do I expect God to bless me because "I'm good?" Do I look for the reward that is coming to me? Do I get discouraged when God rewards others and doesn't reward me?

Week 5 — Day 5 — Posts

Read Esther Chapter 8

Laundry Basket: Esther 8:10-14
Three times in the book of Esther we have read where the posts (couriers) were to deliver the word of the King. They were at the king's beckon call and they were to go with haste to deliver the king's commands. There is no occasion where the posts refuse to go. They willingly do their job. There is great value in their work. They are very important to the functioning of the kingdom.

Laundry Lesson: Ironing is a tedious and demanding task. Every wrinkle, every crease, and every dart pressed just right. At my house always someone is standing over your shoulder waiting for you to finish. Hurry! Mom. But do it right! This is how I feel sometimes about sharing the gospel. Such a sense of urgency but oh, I have to do it right! Thankfully, Jesus will do the talking but we have to do the preparing.

Laundry: Taking the Word

Let's dig into verse 14: *The couriers, riding the royal horses, raced out, spurred on by the king's command. And the edict was also issued in the citadel of Susa.*

Couriers – footman,
        Spurred on – to tremble inwardly, be alarmed or agitated, speedy
Command – decree, message, saying

Other places in scripture couriers (posts) are described as warriors who help out on the battlefield. So these men are those that carry out the word of the King. They go quickly with urgency.

List times when you should have carried the gospel:

_____   _____
_____   _____
_____   _____

Laundry Detergent (God's Word): Fill in the blanks.
Could it be that we are to share our faith in haste because the time of the return of Jesus Christ is at hand? We are commanded to spread the gospel. We are commanded to give account of our faith. We are commanded to lead others to Christ. We are to be God's footman (couriers, posts). We are to be willingly share the faith we have in Jesus. We need to be quick to share what Christ has

done and is doing for us. We need to feel a since of urgency, just like the posts that delivered the word of defense for the Jews. We, as Christians, need to spread the gospel with urgency realizing that a day of destruction for those who do not believe is coming quickly.

II Timothy 4:2 preach the Word; be _____ in season and out of season; correct, rebuke and encourage—with great patience and careful instruction.

Mark 16:15 He said to them, "Go into _____ the world and _____ the good news to _____ creation.

Luke 4:18 The Spirit of the Lord is on me, because he has _____ me to _____ good news to the poor. He has sent me to _____ freedom for the prisoners and recovery of sight for the blind, to _____ the oppressed.

Romans 10:15 And how can they preach unless they are sent? As it is written, "How _____ are the _____ of those who bring good news.

Ephesians 6:15 and with your feet fitted with the _____ that comes from the gospel of peace.

Matthew 10:7 As you go, _____ this message: 'The kingdom of heaven is near.

Luke 9:60 [60]Jesus said to him "Let the dead bury their own dead, but you _____and _____ the kingdom of God."

List 3 people (as God guides) that you would like to share Jesus with this week:
- _____
- _____
- _____

Steam Cleaned:
Lord, help me see the importance of always being ready to share the gospel. Help me have your eyes to see those who need to know you. Show me those you would like for me to share with. Most of all help me live a life that points people to you even if I don't say a word.

In Jesus Name,

Amen

Dirty Laundry (Personal Evaluation):
Am I willing to deliver the word? Do I prepare myself to share Jesus? Do I feel a
sense of urgency about others need for Jesus?

Week 6 — Day 1 — Esther

Read Esther Chapter 8

Laundry Basket: Esther 8:3-6
In these verses, Esther is making petition for her family. Yes, it seems she is asking the same thing she asked in Chapter 7 but there is one significant difference. This time she is asking with urgency. Esther realizes that time is running out. She realizes that there is not much time left for the reversal of the condemnation against the Jews. She knows if something is not done quickly it will be too late. But take notice this is not the first petition for the lives of her people. This is petition number 3. She has asked repeatedly for the lives of her people to be spared. She has not given up. She has not quit. She believes the king is able to make a change and determines to see that he does. She knows that she has no other course of action. The king is the final authority. The king is the only one who can help. Her confidence must be applied to his account.

Laundry Lesson: Ever realize there is a stain on your blouse just a few minutes before you planned to wear it. You make several attempts to get the stain out. You rinse it, you scrub it, and you try what your grandmother taught you. You work feverishly to get the stain removed. Several attempts, no stopping until the blouse is ready to wear without a stain. This is how we should be when we are petitioning the Lord for the salvation of friends and loved ones. One attempt at prayer or one attempt at a conversation with that love one may not be enough. We are talking about a spiritual battle and perseverance must be added in the mix. We must make several attempts. We must work feverishly at prayer for those who are unsaved.

Laundry: Petition for Family

Just like Esther we should not give up after one attempt. We need to realize that, yes, God does hear our prayers and he does answer. But satan is waging war against those who are under conviction. Satan does not want another soul saved. Therefore, on behalf of those unsaved friends and loved ones we must continue to wage a spiritual attack on their behalf. Don't give up because you feel the person will never come to Christ. Remember there is no heart so evil that God cannot change it. We have to continue to petition the Lord for the people's salvation. God is the one that will draw them to salvation so we need always to pray that there will be no obstacles to hinder the salvation of those we know need the Lord.

Esther begged, pleaded and wept for her family. How long has it been since we truly felt the burden to pray and petition God for the salvation of our family and friends? Esther knew time was short. She knew that she had no time to waste. We need to realize that no one is guaranteed tomorrow. No one is promised their next breath. We need to act now. We need to plead with God for the opportunity or someone to have the opportunity to witness those we love and want to see come to know Christ.

We have been sitting back too long waiting for others to lead our friends and family to Christ. We need to be busy about the work of the Kingdom. We shouldn't be "blasting" anyone with the "turn or burn" speech but we do need to be sensitive about the leading of the spirit.

Did you notice also that every time Esther went to the king on behalf of others she was accepted and found favor with the king? How much more will we find acceptance and favor with our Heavenly father.

Let's make ourselves a list of those we need to begin to pray for on a regular basis:

_____

_____

_____

Laundry Detergent (God's Word): Fill in the blanks.
James 4:3: When you _____ you do not receive, because you ask with _____ _____, that you may spend what you get on your pleasures.

Matthew 21:22: If you _____ you will _____ whatever you ask for in prayer."

Luke 11:9: So I say to you: _____ and it will be _____ to you; _____ and you will _____; knock and the door will be _____ to you.

John 11:22: But I know that even now God will _____ you whatever you _____.

John 15:7: If you _____ in me and my _____ remain in you, ask _____ you wish, and it will be _____ you.

John 15:16: [16]You did not _____ me, but I _____ you and appointed you to go and _____ _____—fruit that will last. Then the Father will give you _____ you ask in my name.

I John 5:14-15: This is the _____ we have in approaching God: that if we ask _____ according to his will, he _____ us. [15]And if we know that he hears us—whatever we ask—we know that we have what we asked of him.

So all we have to do is ask. We are praying in his will when we pray for the salvation of others. Pray, Pray, Pray and then go and see what God would have you do to help those you love come to know Christ.

3 steps will you take this week to begin petitioning God for the salvation of your family members:

- _____
- _____
- _____

Steam Cleaned:

Lord, please give me a heart of petition for friends and loved ones that don't know you. Tender the areas of my heart that do not reflect your heart. Give me eyes to see people as you see them and the love for them that would go beyond the surface of "your okay, I'm okay." Help me invest in people so that your love will impact lives and change hearts.

In Jesus Name,
Amen

Dirty Laundry (Personal Evaluation):
Do I pray for lost family and friends, as I should? Do I have a genuine concern for their souls? Have I given God every opportunity to use me?

Week 6 — Day 2 — Jews

Read Esther Chapter 8

Laundry Basket: Esther 8:14-17

In every province and in every city, wherever the edict of the king went, there was joy and gladness among the Jews, with feasting and celebrating. And many people of other nationalities became Jews because fear of the Jews had seized them.

Laundry Lesson: Is your wedding dress sealed away in a protective bag waiting for the day when your daughter will wear that dress to marry the love of her life? I remember when we placed my wedding dress in that air tight seal and tucked it away; there was a sense of sadness, a sense of heaviness because that perfect day had passed. The day my daughter pulls that dress from the sealed package and adorns herself will be a sweet time of unforgettable joy. God's gladness should engulf our hearts in much the same way, when is comes in and takes over the place in our heart that has been scarred by loss or hurt. God's joy comes in and opens the seal we have placed around this hard spot in our hearts and gives us a sweet, unforgettable gladness that, we then, want to share with everyone.

Laundry: Gladness for Mourning

Can you imagine millions of Jews sitting around in sackcloth and ashes, and then, these same Jews rejoicing? What an awesome sight to behold. Their joy was very outwardly expressive and loud, very dramatic, and very thankful. They had been rescued from destruction and now they were alive again. No wonder <u>many</u> became Jews as a result.

Oh, how precious to know, that though our sorrow will last for the night, God's joy (our joy) comes in the morning. God's joy is something that cannot be explained in human terms. Joy from the Lord stretches to lengths we are unable to describe. It can reach the depths of the sea and yet climb the highest mountain. Joy from the Lord is steadfast. It is not something that can be taken from us. When God gives joy for our mourning it is a lasting joy.

Notice that because the Jews turned their mourning and rejoicing toward the one true and living God that others came to know him as a result. How this should teach us a remarkable lesson about our life and how we live for Christ.

List areas where God's joy should be prevalent in your life:

_____   _____
_____   _____

Laundry Detergent (God's Word): Fill in the blank.
Isaiah 51:11: The _____ of the LORD will return. They will enter Zion with singing; _____ joy will crown their heads. Gladness and joy will _____ them, and sorrow and sighing will flee away.

Isaiah 60:20: Your sun will never set again, and your moon will wane no more; the _____ will be your _____ light, and your days of sorrow will end.

Isaiah 61:3: and provide for those who grieve in Zion—to bestow on them a _____ of _____ instead of ashes, the oil of _____ instead of mourning, and a _____ of _____ instead of a spirit of despair. They will be called oaks of righteousness, a planting of the LORD for the display of his splendor.

Matthew 5:4: _____ are those who mourn, for they will be _____.

Oh, what great joy there will be when the pain of this life is over and we walk with Christ in heaven:
Revelation 21:4: He will wipe every tear from their eyes. There will be no more death or mourning or crying or pain, for the old order of things has passed away."

3 steps to put joy into practice in your daily life:
- _____
- _____
- _____

Steam Cleaned:
Lord, where I lack joy please restore joy. Where I lack enthusiasm about your peace and comfort restore it; where I tend to dwell on the hurt instead of the healing change my heart. Help me to be filled with you joy so that others will find you and come to know you because they have seen your joy in me.
In Jesus Name,
Amen

Dirty Laundry (Personal Evaluation):
Do I outwardly express God's joy in my life? Do people truly see <u>joy</u> in me? Have I accepted joy for mourning through God's healing?

Week 6 – Day 3 – Jews

Read Esther Chapter 9

Laundry Basket: Esther 9:2-17
In four different places we find that the Jews "gathered" themselves together. They fought together. They did not stand alone. They worked together. Every time it mentioned the Jews defending themselves it starts out "they gathered themselves together" or "they assembled themselves together." Gathered or assembled carries the same meaning: to convoke, assemble or gather. They came together to fight.

Laundry Lesson: I am one who likes to collect <u>all</u> the dirty clothes, wash <u>all</u> the loads, fold <u>all</u> the loads and then put <u>all</u> the clothes away at one time. Why do the same job 15 different times the same day. Do it all together. It makes the task seem like something has been accomplished. A mountain has been moved. The same with coming together as a body of believers, we accomplish great things when we stand together as a congregation. We can move mountains together.

Laundry: Gathered Together

The Jews stood together as God's chosen people and God was with them and defended them. Just as the Jews, when we stand together in unity God is with us and for us. We need to assemble ourselves together not just for encouragement but also for strength for the battle. Our working together is not just a matter of purpose but a matter of life or destruction.

Could it be that just as the Jews faced a real and physical enemy and they had to stand corporately against it, that we as today's Christians face a real enemy that we need to assemble together and stand against corporately? We draw strength for the day to day fight when we gather together.

List the excuses you make for not gathering for corporate worship or bible study:

---------------------   ---------------------
---------------------   ---------------------
---------------------   ---------------------

Laundry Detergent (God's Word): Fill in the blanks.

Hebrews 10:25: Let us not give up _____ together, as some are in the habit of doing, but let us _____ one another—and all the more as you see the Day approaching.

Proverbs 11:14: For lack of _____ a nation falls, but _____ advisers make victory sure.

Proverbs 15:22: Plans fail for lack of _____, but with _____ advisers they succeed.

Proverbs 24:6: for waging war you need _____, and for victory _____ advisers.

Ecclesiastes 4:9: _____ are better than _____, because they have a _____ return for their _____.

Ecclesiastes 4:11-12: Also, if two lie down together, they will keep warm. But how can one keep warm alone? Though one may be _____, two can _____ themselves. A cord of three strands is _____quickly broken.

Matthew 18:19-20: Again, I tell you that if _____ of you on earth agree about _____you ask for, it will be done for you by my Father in heaven. For where two or three come _____ in my name, there am I with them.

What changes will you make to be ready for the corporate battle:
- _____
- _____
- _____

Steam Cleaned:
Lord, help me not to make excuses about being ready for battle in the corporate body of Christ. Help me to realize that I can not fight the enemy without others to help. Cause my heart to be softened to the struggles and battles of others that I might come along side them and fight with and for them.

In Jesus Name,

Amen

Dirty Laundry (Personal Evaluation):
Do I join with the body of Christ to gain strength for the battle? Do I help form a united front against the enemy? Is my armor fit for battle in the collective fight? Am I a prayer warrior for the corporate battle of the congregation?

Week 6 — Day 4 — Jews

Read Esther Chapter 9

Laundry Basket: Esther 9:2-5

Can you see the hand of God in this? Do you see that God's provision for his chosen people took the enemy with the most power and turned it into a link in the defense?

Laundry Lesson: Ever heard of using cat litter on a grease stain. It works! Place the cat litter on the stain for a few hours and it will soak up the grease. My first thought: "I need to wash both out of my clothes." Both seem to be something that needs cleaning out, but in reality one helps get rid of the other. That's what happens when God takes control and turns our enemies into our defense. He takes what we want to have removed from our lives and makes them a strength that we need.

Laundry: Enemies to Advocates

Esther 9:3 and all the nobles of the provinces, the satraps, the governors and the king's administrators helped the Jews, because fear of Mordecai had seized them.

Because of Mordecai's reputation and God's intervention the Jews did not suffer destruction.

List areas where you need God to bring an advocate to your side:

_____   _____
_____   _____
_____   _____

Laundry Detergent (God's Word):

The story of Esther is not the only time in scripture that the enemy turned to advocate.

✝ Read Acts 16:23-40 and then answer the following questions:

Was the jailor on Paul and Silas' defense at the beginning?

_____

What caused the jailor to change his point of view?

The jailor went from enemy (guard) to brother in Christ. His heart was turned because of the reputation of Paul and Silas. God caused an earthquake; the jailor got literally shaken to his core. He didn't understand what was happening around him. Then Paul and Silas let their faith and their God speak. They did not leave when they had the opportunity to escape from prison. They left an impression by their actions. The jailor then became a Christian.

✝ Read Daniel Chapter 3 then answer the following questions:

Who was Shadrach, Meshach, and Abednego's enemy?

What was their punishment for not bowing down?

Why did the king change his mind about the God of Shadrach, Meshach, and Abednego? _____

_____

At the end of Chapter 3 the king has totally changed his position. What happened to Shadrach, Meshach, and Abednego?

Mordecai, Paul, Silas, Shadrach, Meshach, and Abednego were all men that stood for what was right. They were all faithful to the Lord. They knew where their strength and provision was found. They all had spotless reputations. Their behavior matched their speech. They were men sold out to God. They rested entirely on his provision.

List 3 enemies God has turned to advocate for you:
- _____
- _____
- _____

Steam Cleaned:
Lord, please help me understand that there are people and situations in my life that you are working for my good and your glory. Help me to recognize that though right now I may have those in my life that seem like enemies that you are working those same people to be my advocates. Help me trust you and you only. Convict me where my reputation does not represent you well and cause me to change my attitude and actions to reflect your heart.   *In Jesus Name, Amen*

Dirty Laundry (Personal Evaluation):
Do I allow God to work out the defense system he would like to use for me? Can I see God turning an enemy into a defender? Am I patient enough to allow all things to work for good? Do I believe God can turn my enemies to my advocates?

Week 6 — Day 5 — Jews
Read Esther Chapter 9

Laundry Basket: Esther 9:17-32
Purim is a time of celebration and feasting in the Jewish community even today. These days were established as a remembrance to the Jewish people. They were to remember that evil was meant for them and God delivered them from the hands of their enemies.

Laundry Lesson: I tried a new detergent just a few weeks ago and as I stood taking the clothes from the washer the fragrance coming from the clothes reminded me of something from my childhood. It smelled like push-up popsicles that we would buy from the ice cream man. We were only allowed to get them on special occasions. That smell brought back lots of memories. Our spiritual markers should do the same for our spiritual senses. There should be things and people that remind us of the spiritual activity that has taken place in our lives. These makers should cause us to remember God's faithfulness and his protection over us.

Laundry: Remembrance

The name Purim came from the casting of lots; the casting of lots is called "Pur.". In the Greek when a word is made plural you add an "im". (Ex: So cherub become cherubim) So to remember the "pur" was cast to determine the day on which the Jews were to be destroyed, they made it a celebration of "Purim."

Three days before the celebration of Purim begins, the Jews will go on a fast. To commemorate the fast Esther had before going to the King.

On the first day of Purim, the Jews send food to the neighbors and friends; it is to be a token of remembrance of provision. They will exchange one food. Then in the evening they will have a feast.

The second day of Purim the Jews will dress in costume and have a parade. When evening comes and time for the feast, the father will read the story of Esther. Anytime Esther or Mordecai's names are mentioned everyone cheers and claps. Anytime Haman's name is mentioned the Jews spit on the ground and boo.
Purim is all about remembrance. It is about remembering God's providence and provision. We celebrate times of remembrance also: Easter, Christmas,

Memorial Day, Independence Day, President's Day, Martin Luther King Day, birthdays and anniversaries. These all have special meaning to us and we celebrate by remembering. Having a time of remembrance is good. It causes us to focus on the important deliverances or victories in our lives.

List spiritual milestones in you life:

_____   _____
_____   _____
_____   _____

Laundry Detergent (God's Word): Fill in the blanks.
Exodus 20:8: Remember the _____ _____ by keeping it holy.

Numbers 15:40: Then you will remember to _____ all my _____ and will be _____ to your God.

Deuteronomy 32:7: Remember the _____ _____ _____; _____ the generations long past. Ask your _____ and he will tell you, your elders, and they will _____ to you.

I Chronicles 16:12: Remember the _____ he has done, his _____, and the _____ he pronounced.

Psalm 77:11: I will remember the _____ of the LORD; yes, I will remember your _____ of long ago.

Psalm 143:5: remember the days of long ago; I _____ on all your _____ and consider what your _____ have done.

Luke 22:19: ¹⁹And he took _____, gave thanks and broke it, and gave it to them, saying, "This is my _____ given for you; do this in remembrance of _____."

John 14:26: But the Counselor, the Holy Spirit, whom the Father will send in my name, will _____ you all things and will remind you of _____ I have said to you.

II Timothy 2:8: Remember Jesus Christ, _____ from the dead, _____from David. This is ____ gospel.

God calls us to remembrance. He wants us to remember him, his works and his provision for us. Remembrance strengthens our faith; it causes us to walk a much straighter path with him.

God remembers!!!

He also forgets:

Genesis 9:15: I will remember my _____ between me and you and all living creatures of every kind. _____ again will the waters become a flood to destroy _____ _____.

Hebrews 8:12: For I will _____ their wickedness and will remember their _____no more.

Hebrews 10:17: Then he adds: "Their _____ and _____ acts I will remember no more.

Just as the Jews celebrate and remember their past successes <u>with God</u>, we are to remember and hold fast to the things of God. When God makes a promise, **he remembers**. He is not slack concerning his children. But when we sin **he forgets**. If only we loved and lived that way.

What steps will you take to be sure to pass godly remembrances on to your children:
- _____
- _____
- _____

Steam Cleaned:

Oh God, cause me to remember your activity in my life. Help me to be quick to remember your ways and your workings and quick to forget wrongs done against me. Cause me to pass down to my children the faithfulness that you have had concerning us. Make me daily aware of your presence and to be thankful and mindful of it. Thank you for your continued working and dealing with me so as to cause me to remember and to hold fast to you.

In Jesus Name,

Amen

Dirty Laundry (Personal Evaluation):

As we complete our time learning the character traits from the book of Esther, spend this last time of personal evaluation asking God to reveal the type of "remembrance" (legacy) is going to be left for those to follow. Do I celebrate or rehash my past? Do remembrances bring joy or heartache? Am I making memories or "dirty laundry" for my children, friends, and family?